THE RESOURCEFUL TEACHER Series

Tessa Woodward

THINKING IN THE EFL CLASS

Activities for blending language learning and thinking

Thinking in the EFL Class
by Tessa Woodward

© HELBLING LANGUAGES 2011
www.helblinglanguages.com

All rights reserved; no part of this publication may be reproduced, stored in a retrieval system, or transmitted in any form or by any means, electronic, mechanical, photocopying, recording, or otherwise, without the prior written permission of the Publishers.

Photocopying of materials from this book for classroom use is permitted.

First published 2011
ISBN 978-3-85272-333-4

Edited by Jane Arnold
Copy edited by Caroline Petherick
Designed by Gabby Design
Cover design by Capolinea
Illustrated by Phillip Burrows
Printed by Athesia

Every effort has been made to trace the owners of any copyright material in this book.
If notified, the publisher will be pleased to rectify any errors or omissions.

To Bella

Acknowledgements

Thanks to Seth, my husband, for everything including first listening to this manuscript and then reading it.

Thanks to all the staff at Helbling Languages for their flexibility, speed, and sheer positive spirit. It is a wonderful feeling to have people committed to helping you make a book better.

Contents

	Introduction		9
CHAPTER 1:	**FUNDAMENTALS**		21
	TT1	Building an atmosphere for thinking	23
	TT2	Responding to student questions and contributions	23
	TT3	Finding out what we really do	24
	TT4	Types of teacher questions	24
	TT5	Answering our own questions	25
	TT6	Wait-time	25
	TT7	Echoing	26
	TT8	Follow-up questions	27
	TT9	Roadblocks to communication	27
	TT10	Being positive	29
	TT11	Getting the target language into the room	30
	TT12	Class routines	30
	TT13	Moving students around	30
	TT14	While you are busy	31
	TT15	Finishing lessons off	31
	1.1	Invent a handshake	32
	1.2	Simply stimulate	33
	1.3	Counting games	34
	1.4	Expanding a sentence	36
	1.5	Clem's spiral (and other one-minute activities)	37
	1.6	The learning dip and rise	39
	1.7	My favourite mistakes	41
	1.8	Just one good thing	43
	1.9	'Menu' on the board	44
	1.10	Concept map … a true advance organiser	46
	1.11	Crazy Questions *or* 'Thunks'	48
	1.12	Puzzles	50
	1.13	Labelling the room	52
	1.14	Grammarless beginnings	54
	1.15	Taking the register	57
	1.16	Solo silent reflection	59
	1.17	Keyword group mapping	60
	1.18	What? How? Why?	61
	1.19	Transfer	62
CHAPTER 2:	**BUILDING CONCEPTS, LOOKING FOR PATTERNS AND MEMORISING**		65
	TT1	Building concepts	67
	TT2	Looking for patterns	69
	TT3	Memorising	70
	2.1	Learning a language is like …?	71
	2.2	Question matrix	73
	2.3	Concept sheets	75

Contents

2.4	Concept stretching	77
2.5	Refining vocabulary	79
2.6	Things of this shape	81
2.7	Small collections	83
2.8	Clap, listen, clap	85
2.9	Odd one(s) out	86
2.10	Like WHAT??!!	89
2.11	Physical storage	91
2.12	Mnemonics	93
2.13	Rehearsal	95
2.14	Mime round the circle	96
2.15	Eight-step memorising procedure	97
2.16	Guided picture composition	100

CHAPTER 3: KEEPING IT PRACTICAL: WAYS OF STRUCTURING LESSONS FOR THINKING — 103

TT1	Thinking that is fundamental to language learning	105
TT2	Unusual teacher reflection	105
TT3	The English National Curriculum approach	105
TT4	Exploratory talk: the use of language for thinking together	107
TT5	Imaginative Education	109
TT6	Making the learning of English heroic	110
3.1	Exploratory talk ground rules	113
3.2	Gathering exploratory talk language	114
3.3	Doing exploratory talk	115
3.4	Inspiring people	116
3.5	Behold the humble button!	118

CHAPTER 4: USING EVERYDAY THINKING FRAMEWORKS — 121

TT1	Listing	123
TT2	Reversals	123
4.1	Rules for a good society	125
4.2	I'm grateful for …	127
4.3	True or false *or* Facts and myths	128
4.4	How times have changed!	129
4.5	Are we the same or different?	131
4.6	List poems	133
4.7	Right name wrong name	135
4.8	That's not right! *or* 'Cinderfella'	136
4.9	Reversals anecdotes	138
4.10	Working backwards from goals	140
4.11	Fortunately, unfortunately	142
4.12	Change the text	144
4.13	Flip it and see	146

Contents

CHAPTER 5:	CREATIVE THINKING		149
	TT1	Being prolific	151
	TT2	Creating unusual or novel combinations	151
	TT3	Making thinking visible	151
	TT4	Using generative frameworks	151
	TT5	Building empathy	152
	5.1	Creativity brainstorm	153
	5.2	You can use it to …	155
	5.3	Just one colour	156
	5.4	Thirty things I did	157
	5.5	Picture pack plethora	158
	5.6	Checking vocabulary many ways	160
	5.7	Comparing a text and a picture	161
	5.8	If she were an animal, she'd be a panther!	162
	5.9	Scrabble word review	164
	5.10	Musical post cards	166
	5.11	Graphic organiser variety	168
	5.12	Inventing new buttons	172
	5.13	Potato talks	174
	5.14	Acrostics	176
	5.15	Two similarities, two differences	178
	5.16	I am one among many	179
	5.17	Questions to the head	181
	5.18	What are they really thinking?	183
	5.19	Half a conversation	185
	5.20	Your festival or mine?	187
CHAPTER 6:	THINKING CLEARLY ABOUT TEXTS AND SITUATIONS		191
	TT1	Stories	193
	6.1	Where does it come from?	195
	6.2	Balancing the books	197
	6.3	Fact or opinion?	199
	6.4	Spot the smuggled mistake!	202
	6.5	Which text is right?	205
	6.6	Through my eyes *or* Am I biased?	207
	6.7	General knowledge building	209
	6.8	What's the right thing to do?	212
	6.9	Which proverb is right?	216
	6.10	Should I do what I am told by famous people?	218
	6.11	Learning from stories	220
	6.12	Thinking clearly about problems	223

Contents

CHAPTER 7:		DESIGNING TASKS AND ACTIVITIES TO ENCOURAGE THINKING	227
	TT1	Removing restrictions from activities	229
	TT2	Adding restrictions to activities	230
	TT3	Using classroom formats that encourage thinking and sharing of ideas	232
	TT4	Choosing interesting themes and material types	235
	TT5	Using imagination and fantasy	236
	7.1	The Museum of Curiosities	237
	7.2	Room 101	239

Further reading   241

Teacher's quick-reference guide   245

Introduction

Thinking is as natural as breathing and drinking. We do it all the time. In fact it is almost impossible to choose *not* to do it! While some of our thinking pleases us, making us feel fresh, making us smile, there are other times when our thoughts are repetitive or negative and worrying. The good thing is that just as we can learn different ways of breathing so that we can support a singing voice or slow our breathing down to help us relax, and we can learn a different way of drinking for when we sip to taste a fine wine, so we can learn different kinds of thinking for different purposes.

We might feel, generally in life, that if we are in a very routine situation, we don't really need to do lot of productive thinking. But even in the most routine of lives, we may be faced with unpredictability in employment, in population migration, in the breakdown of family or health, or in environmental, political and technological change. So, even when we are not deliberately setting out to learn something new, we often need to keep alert and to think clearly, critically and compassionately.

In our work in the EFL class, teachers and students do lots of thinking. We are involved in understanding or explaining concepts, noticing similarities and differences, looking for patterns, committing to memory and endeavouring to achieve fast recall. In class, we are all also involved in self-management. We try, for example, not to panic when we don't understand something. We try to muster patience when we can't express what we want. We try not to worry when we get puzzling reactions to our work.

'Thinking' is a big topic. So is 'Thinking in education', a subject which has become very popular recently, for there has been a movement advocating the teaching of thinking. It is my aim in this book to harness this movement in a way that is fruitful to EFL/ESL/ESOL teachers and students. Most EFL state school teachers and most adult education teachers are in settings that limit our ability to change our curriculum. We need ways of working with thinking that are realistic and doable in our everyday situations.

One way of getting into any big topic is to ask a large number of basic questions first and to come up with some initial answers. That way, we can start to lay out the perimeters of the field and to chart a path through it. So, below, I have done just that with the topic of thinking in the EFL class. You may well want to add other questions, and you may have different answers to my questions.

FUNDAMENTAL QUESTIONS ABOUT THINKING IN THE EFL CLASS

What is thinking?

If we asked a thousand people this question, we'd probably get a thousand different answers. Everything from 'It's the cerebral manipulation of information' to 'It's the way we represent the world in our heads and deal with it according to our plans' to 'It's how we understand things, solve problems and make decisions' to 'It's what goes through my head and makes me feel excited and richer!'

In lay terms, what different types of thinking do we recognise?

If we look at some of the huge number of alternative words we have in English for the verb 'to think', we can see the sorts of thinking that we feel we know about:

Consider, ponder, reflect, surmise, judge, daydream, imagine, dream up, dwell on, mull over, contemplate, meditate, brood, assume, presume, suppose, figure out, analyse, infer, deduce, interpret, hypothesise, determine, formulate, realise, empathise and *philosophise* ...

And then we also have phrases like: *positive thinking, lateral thinking, critical thinking, thinking out loud, wishful thinking, creative thinking* and *thinking for yourself*, and expressions such as *to think twice, to have a train of thought, to be lost in thought, to be a right-brain thinker* and *Stop thinking about it and sleep on it!*

In everyday life we use these expressions to describe a marvellous variety of mental moves, some conscious and some not. In the world of education, we perhaps tend to use the word 'think', as when a teacher says 'Now I want you all to think about ...', to mean a rather more conscious and goal-directed process. I would rather retain a wider perspective in this book. Bruner described learning as a multifaceted process in which emotions, thoughts and actions do not occur in isolation, but are aspects of a larger, unified whole. He suggested that drawing heavy conceptual boundaries between thought, action and emotion would only require us to construct conceptual bridges later, connecting what should never have been separated in the first place. He argued that people are 'perfinkers'; that is they perceive, feel and think all at once (Bruner 1986: 118). I'll try to hold on to this understanding as I go through the book.

In language learning what different types of thinking are important?

I am sure you will be able to add to my list but it seems to me that the following must be important. So, just for starters, what about these?
>Scanning and manipulating data, noticing patterns, comparing and contrasting, recognising categories and odd ones out, researching and evaluating the credibility of sources, selecting from options according to context, diagnosing problems, marshalling solutions and selecting the best, understanding principles and transferring them to new situations, accepting and following rules, devising mnemonics, memorising, recalling, predicting, deducing, inferring, creating, imagining, reflecting on what has been learned and how, understanding feedback and deciding what to do about it, and organising time and resources.

And as for self-management skills, we could perhaps include:
Control of anxiety, being patient and calm, having self-belief, paying attention, co-operating with peers, keeping a sense of humour, working under a leader, judging the type and level of participation required, challenging yourself, taking risks, working alone, prioritising, pacing yourself, setting goals, being flexible, persevering and exploring.

Are there some core thinking tasks we do in many different domains?

Yes. In the domains of practical everyday life, in educational disciplines, and in many different jobs we all very often have, for example, to:
Plan, identify, define and analyse problems, generate creative alternatives, critique ideas, resolve conflict through negotiation, look for patterns of recurrence, create mnemonics, evaluate the reliability of information sources, analyse, synthesise, design things, debate, and imagine how others feel.

We can get better at all these things in one subject area. Then, if we think about them explicitly and transfer what we have learned, we can perhaps get better at applying them in other areas too.

What could it mean to be a 'better' thinker?

A Buddhist might say it means to think skilfully so that we end up calm, focused and happy and thus able to wholeheartedly support our own actions. An employer might say it means becoming more efficient, effective, and good in a team as well as being able to come up with fresh ideas when faced with tricky, old situations or tricky, new, atypical ones. My niece might say it means becoming more ethical and ecological.

Someone who has thought a lot about the teaching of thinking, such as Smith (2004), might say a good thinker would have a firm grasp of concepts, principles and other declarative knowledge, have good mental habits, know how to perform certain mental activities well, would use discretion and judgement and be sensitive to the context of application, and would be aware of their own values and dispositions.[1]

And as to those good mental habits mentioned above, Professor Arthur L. Costa might say it means skilfully and mindfully employing 'habits of mind'. Costa defines habits of mind as 'dispositions that are employed when we are confronted with problems the solutions to which are not immediately apparent'. Costa and Kallick (2000) have identified 16 habits of mind:
- persisting, thinking and communicating with clarity and precision
- managing impulsivity

---

[1] *I would personally say that being a better thinker would mean being more flexible, being able to make important decisions, making the best use of our talents and resources, dealing with more and more complex content and maybe even fighting less! Overall, we could hope it might mean being a successful learner, a thoughtful citizen and a more confident and imaginative person.*

- gathering data through all senses
- listening with understanding and empathy
- creating, imaging and innovating
- thinking flexibly
- responding with wonderment and awe
- thinking about thinking (i.e. metacognition)
- taking responsible risks
- striving for accuracy
- finding humour
- questioning and posing problems
- thinking interdependently
- applying past knowledge to new situations
- remaining open to continuous learning.

Are there any widely accepted taxonomies or frameworks of different kinds of thinking?

You may well have heard of de Bono's lateral thinking tools, of Howard Gardner's theory of multiple intelligences or of Bloom's taxonomy. Many authors such as Ausubel (1968), Feuerstein (1980), Gagne (1985) and Romiszowski (1981) have tried to bring clarity and order to the complex topic of thinking, especially to that of the thinking processes necessary for learning. Many useful lists, frameworks, taxonomies and models of the cognitive, emotional and social aspects of thinking have been devised. Moseley et al (2005) give an excellent overview of 41 such major frameworks, including all the ones mentioned above so far. Of course, as language teachers simply trying to keep ourselves and our students mentally fresh, we do not have to choose any of these 41 frameworks. If we do decide to turn to one of the major taxonomies, we should choose one that helps us to do what we want to do, realising that they were all devised for different purposes. My main purpose in this book is practical, though, so I am personally much more interested in what will support busy, working teachers to keep things fresh in class and less so in presenting and discussing theoretical frameworks and terminological distinctions.

What would be an example of one of these taxonomies?

Apart from Costa and Kallick, 2000, mentioned above, a very well-known classification of educational objectives is the one produced by a committee of college and university examiners, led by Benjamin Bloom, in 1956. The committee identified three domains of educational activities:
- **cognitive**: involving mental abilities (aka *knowledge*)
- **affective**: about growth in feelings or emotional areas (aka *attitude*)
- **psychomotor**: about development of manual or physical skills (aka *skills*).

The committee fleshed out the cognitive and affective domains quite fully, but less information was offered on the psychomotor domain.

There are six hierarchical levels in the cognitive part of the taxonomy. These are listed below, starting with the so-called 'lower order' thinking processes or skills, often referred to as 'LOTS', and moving to the 'higher order' ones, often nicknamed 'HOTS'.

LOTS
1. Knowledge
    - Knowledge of specifics such as terminology and specific facts.
    - Knowledge of ways and means of dealing with specifics – so, conventions, trends and sequences, classifications and categories, criteria and methodology.
    - Knowledge of the universals and abstractions in a field, i.e. principles and generalisations, theories and structures.
2. Comprehension
   Demonstrative understanding of facts and ideas by organising, comparing, translating, interpreting, giving descriptions, and stating main ideas and extrapolating from them.
3. Application
   Using new knowledge to, e.g., solve problems by applying acquired knowledge in a different way.

HOTS
4. Analysis
   Examining and breaking down notions into their:
    - elements
    - relationships
    - organisational principles.
5. Synthesis
   Compiling information in a different way by putting elements together in a new pattern, or proposing alternative solutions as in, for example, the production of a unique communication, plan, or proposed set of operations.
6. Evaluation
   Presenting and defending opinions by making judgments in terms of
    - internal evidence
    - external criteria.

Is it possible to teach ways of thinking?

Whether we are trying to get our students to notice a language pattern or to work with them on something like 'evaluation' from Bloom's taxonomy above, we can provide a rich, supportive, interesting and imaginative environment with plenty of opportunities to think and learn, and plenty of interesting content to think about. We can check frequently on how things are going and then ... hope that learning happens, and see if it has! Thinking and learning take place within a body and a life, within a group, and a culture, so it is hard to prove exactly what it is we have taught or what is actually learned and why and how.

Is teaching thinking a new idea?

No. In education there have been many moves to teach thinking. We know that Socrates, for example, deliberately employed special kinds of questions to draw his students towards interesting conclusions and away from traditional ones. In more recent times, we have had movements such as Philosophy for Children (P4C), and Critical Thinking (CT). What these have in common is the belief that different kinds of thinking *can* be taught or enhanced in all ages and types of students, and that overtly working on thinking improves academic achievement, gives us gains in learning and increases student participation as well as keeping teachers professionally motivated.

What *is* definitely new is the huge increase in information and messages many of us enjoy or suffer each day via print and electronic media. We have to learn how to deal with this multiplicity. In the words of the poem 'Snow' by Louis MacNeice, we often 'feel the drunkenness of things being various'.

When campaigning for the US presidency in July of 2008, Barack Obama was talking to David Cameron, and said, 'Should we be successful, actually the most important thing you need to do is to have big chunks of time during the day when all you're doing is thinking. Without that, you lose the big picture.'

Does age make a difference to learning new ways of thinking?

We used to think that children had several distinct developmental stages and thus could not learn certain things before certain ages. Piaget, the founder of this theory, being a biologist, was definitely on the right track. He was, however, working before knowledge of neuro-transmission, before brain scanning technology and other developments in cognitive science. We now tend to think of child development as more of a continuum than a set of hard and fast phases.

We also used to believe that we were born with a finite number of brain cells that were gradually destroyed over our life time, leaving us, by the age of 60, old dogs unable to learn new tricks. However, research by Sherry Willis[2] on the value of mental workouts in boosting reasoning skills, memory, and mental processing is more hopeful. The commonsense 'Use it or lose it!' slogan is also relevant here.

Aren't teachers of languages already involved in teaching thinking?

Yes. As I mentioned above, learning a language is a highly complex cognitive task involving working out grammar rules, spotting similarities and differences between different spoken and written forms, understanding norms of use, appropriacy, and cultural constraints, and memorising, plus an immense amount of self-management, just for starters. Teaching a foreign language also involves the ability to break down and lay out concepts, to plan the interaction of time, content,

---

2 *The Gerontology Centre, Penn State University (reported by Shankar Vedantam in the Washington Post December 20, 2006).*

materials, space and students, to reflect, to adapt, and to judge and assess. As language teachers and learners, we are thus already involved in huge amounts of complex thinking. We can choose to do this work without referring to it at a meta-level. We can, alternatively, choose to pull this type of work into the foreground and make it overt and more effective by talking with students about the fact that they are, for example, learning to 'notice' something (e.g. that in English regular verbs have 'ed' added to them in the Past Simple tense) and that 'noticing' is a kind of thinking that is very important in language learning.

How else could teachers of languages get involved in teaching thinking?

In the EFL class we work with all kinds of topics. We might use a story about a bear, or a text about holidays or a listening exercise about chocolate. We don't usually dwell that much on the topic other than making sure students find it interesting, can comprehend it, perhaps discuss it and learn its related vocabulary and structures. We could thus equally well use an occasional text on a thinking topic, e.g. about useful ways of memorising vocabulary. Or we could have a lesson that involves doing research to prepare for a debate. Or students could do a warm-up exercise involving problem-solving techniques. Again, we could do any of these without drawing too much attention to them or, alternatively, we could flag them all up and point out to students that the topic or content was actually connected to useful mental habits and ways of thinking.

Another way of working would be to look at our lay understanding of different kinds of thinking such as philosophising, or at our list of types of thinking connected to language learning (see above) or at one of the many taxonomies available (e.g. Bloom), and choose to teach elements of it in a regular and systematic way, in English. This would actually be a kind of Content and Language Integrated Learning or CLIL. Students would, in this hypothetical situation, acquire a new language (English), and learn a lot about a new topic (different ways of thinking) at the same time. They could be made aware that they were learning two things at once. A kind of 'Buy One Get One Free!'

Those working in primary or secondary schools might also say that we have a responsibility to prepare our students not just for communication in a foreign language but also for other aspects of their future. We might then say we are responsible for foreign language learning and also, partly, for 'life skills'. We could thus cordon off part of our lessons or part of the school curriculum for this sort of work. The class activities done in lessons on related movements such as Philosophy for Children (P4C) and Critical Thinking are usually seen as part of separate subjects in a school curriculum in this way.

Looking at it in yet another way, if a nation, region or institution is totally committed to the principle of children learning how to think, then attempts will be made to integrate the teaching of thinking skills throughout a whole school curriculum. In this type of curriculum, teachers of subjects such as geography and history will all gradually integrate the teaching of thinking skills into their classes! An example here is in the National Curriculum of England. Five thinking 'skills' (information-processing, reasoning, enquiry, creative thinking and evaluation) are to be taught to learners in every school subject including modern foreign languages in secondary schools in the UK. (More on this in chapter 3, TT3.)

The teaching tips (TTs) in the first part of each chapter in this book will be useful to a teacher of any language. But the activities in the second part of each chapter and for use with students are written specifically for EFL teachers. Thus if you teach a different modern language, you will need to rethink the language examples.

Do all these different ways of working have implications for the way we plan lessons?

Yes, and these implications are also discussed in chapter 3.

What is the point of this deliberate integration of work on useful ways of thinking with language learning?

The advantages seen by proponents are many. It is thought that:
- Working on thinking is inherently interesting and so makes good content for a language lesson.
- It also encourages learners to *want* to communicate and to express themselves, and so increases student motivation and participation. The language they produce can then be worked on.
- Good thinkers make good language learners. Teaching thinking should thus enhance language learning and achievement.
- It helps language teachers to keep intellectually stimulated and to model learning to our learners.
- It helps us to find out what students know and how they are learning, and thus to identify gaps and misconceptions in their learning.
- It helps us language teachers to look at our subject in a new light and to consider different topics and categorisations, thus to 'make new' the familiar.
- It helps us to see beyond subject boundaries and to forge links with professionals in parallel or very different subjects.

Are there any disadvantages to integrating the teaching of thinking into language lessons?

Possibly. Since in language teaching our subject is not just the content of our work but also the vehicle for it, we have to be careful not to spend too much time talking in the mother tongue *about* the target language and *about* thinking. We need to make sure that we spend most of our time *in* the target language. This is still doable if we use efficient ways of working, and *if* we decide to teach our students the language of meta-cognition we do so bit by bit and not all in one go.

What is a likely student response to overt work on thinking?

If we simply do a little work on thinking in the same way as we might use a text on the Australian Open tennis tournament or run a creative writing exercise about ghost stories, students will probably not notice much of a change. They will simply let us know in their usual ways whether they did or didn't enjoy a particular topic or activity on the subject of thinking. If we choose a more sustained approach, then a student who has done really well within a transmission style of teaching (where there is one right answer that is usually fed in by the teacher) might find the change harder to adjust to. Students who enjoy a less 'mug and jug' approach, on the other hand, may well show greater interest in these new activities and lessons, where they can come up with surprising ideas that they themselves enjoy. Their motivation might well improve.

Some of the students I teach are bottom stream. They don't regard themselves as very clever and certainly don't know anything about philosophy or logic.

This is really not a problem in terms of this book. No prior knowledge of any kind of thinking is assumed or necessary. I offer some ways of building a good atmosphere and some activities which will help students to attend, to notice things, be a little more prolific, have a few more ideas, and learn how to explore ideas with fellow students. I hope the students will enjoy the activities and end up with a little more confidence in their own ability to think.

So what can we busy language teachers do to improve thinking in our own classes?

You probably don't have the time to undertake a PhD on 40 thinking taxonomies and their applications, don't want to throw out all your old materials and ideas, and cannot put aside large blocks of time in your schedule for special philosophy or critical thinking classes.
If, however, you want to prioritise useful language work, practise the types of thinking needed in language learning, use interesting content, and need clear procedures and ways of working, and are also happy to work on things that have definite value outside class and school, then whatever context you are teaching in, this book provides many activities to try.

How can we assess the quality of thinking in our classes?

Traditional exams, no matter how well written they are, do have a tendency to evaluate the more reproductive of students' skills. They check how well a student has understood something and perhaps how well they can summarise that understanding. To test student ability to think clearly, critically and compassionately in a formal way, we would have to come up with novel stimuli and situations or scenarios for an exam, or require extended pieces of work that ask students to do things like analysing, creating, discussing and coming to conclusions and decisions. This kind of specialised testing is outside the scope of this book. Instead, the book contains references to discussions of the quality of thinking students are involved in.

The structure of this book

Chapter One looks at the fundamental things that we teachers can do to avoid blocking our students and, instead, support them as they settle down, think and learn.

Chapter Two works on three types of thinking of maximum relevance to language learning. These are: building concepts, looking for patterns and memorising.

Chapter Three looks back on the work in this introduction, and chapters one and two, and considers what difference their contents might make to lesson structure and planning. It goes on to focus on lesson structures which would be useful if you want to deliberately work with a kind of thinking included in one of the major taxonomies or with imaginative education. It also explains what 'exploratory talk' is and how to achieve it with students.

Chapter Four shows how you can play with simple thinking frameworks such as 'listing' and 'reversals' to give students mental exercise.

Chapter Five deals with creative thinking. How can we practise it? Ideas are grouped under four basic principles.

Chapter Six is about helping students to think clearly about texts and situations. How can students check the provenance and balance of texts, and sort out true facts from mistakes and opinions? How can they go beyond uncritical acceptance of proverbs and inspiring quotations? How can they build their general knowledge, learn from stories and think clearly about problematic situations?

Chapter Seven shares ideas on how we can design tasks and activities to encourage thinking.

This book is about how we teachers can keep our own thinking fresh and how we can help students to think clearly, critically and compassionately. It's about how we can, without massively changing our materials and activities, encourage students of English as a foreign, other or second language to build concepts, notice patterns, memorise, use talk to explore, employ everyday mental frameworks in interesting ways, come up with creative ideas, and think clearly about texts. It is thus an attempt to *meld* the teaching of language with a concern to encourage thinking in classes, without forgetting the importance of general knowledge and interesting content.

Each of the seven following chapters is divided into two parts. The first part, containing sections marked with the symbol 'TT' for 'Teaching Tips', describes steps that you might like to take to help you put more of an emphasis on thinking in your EFL classes. Some of these tips involve practical changes, some are more attitudinal in nature and some encourage you to have a good ponder outside class.

The second part of each chapter contains descriptions of activities that you can use with your classes. In each case the ideas are laid out in recipe format so that for each one you can see its focus, the level of class it is aimed at, the time it will take, materials / preparation, in-class steps, follow-up ideas or variations and any useful notes.

In this introduction I have charted a path through what is potentially a very complex area and have explained the background to my own approach to the subject of thinking in the EFL class. Now, over to you! I really hope you enjoy the thinking and doing implied in the following pages.

 Handouts are downloadable in both PDF and DOC format at www.helblinglanguages.com/thinking/downloads.

CHAPTER 1
FUNDAMENTALS

This chapter looks at the fundamentals we need to cover in order to promote thinking in our classes.
In the Teaching Tips section, I deal with how we can either build a good atmosphere for thinking or, alternatively, block it! We consider the importance of being positive, getting the target language into the classroom as early as possible and keeping routines fresh and creative. In the second section there are activities for you to use with your students to wake them up or calm them down, to help them be realistic about language learning and to stay positive, to look forward to what they are going to do, to think up ideas, to start working naturally in English as soon as possible and, finally, to look back over what they have been learning and to recognise its value.

Teaching Tips
How teachers can set up a thinking atmosphere

 Building an atmosphere for thinking

Let's start with the general tone or mood of a class. A teacher's routines can sometimes become rather mechanical and the energy level a bit low if people block each other's ideas and initiatives. At other times both teacher and students feel lively, get interested, have a lot to say and enjoy each other's ideas. It's hard to put a finger on what exactly makes the difference. But being warm and encouraging, having high expectations of students, and giving students the freedom to express opinions, to explore and take risks are all mentioned in the research literature as really important if we want our students to be brave enough to participate well.

When searching for advice on how exactly to achieve this kind of warm and encouraging classroom climate, one that stimulates thinking, I came across two lists of recommended teacher behaviours which I've adapted and melded below. These are some of the things we can make sure we do:
- set/negotiate ground rules with our students well in advance and display these on the classroom wall
- provide well-planned, interesting activities and content
- find out our students' goals and reasons for learning English and share our goals with them so that they find the work we do meaningful
- challenge students with tasks a little above their current level of competence
- reassure students that, with help, they can do these tasks
- show respect for each student and accept individual differences
- be flexible and positive
- show that we are thinking, learning, taking risks, getting stuck and making mistakes too and that this is okay
- allow students to be active participants
- acknowledge every response
- create success-oriented experiences that are doable at least in part by each student
- help students to connect new learning with old, with other subjects, and with real life
- vary our methods.

(Based on Thacker in Gough, 1991, and Lin and Mackay, 2004.)

TT2 **Responding to student questions and contributions**

In the list above, encouraging students to be active is mentioned. How can we, practically, do this? Well, one way for students to be active is by asking questions. We can encourage our students to ask questions in different ways. We can put a slot onto our timetable labelled *Student Questions*. We can allow time for pairs to talk and write down a question. We can then gather all these questions in and have a look at them. We can discuss them openly with students, thinking together about the types of questions they are and how best they could be answered.

Sometimes, when a student asks a tricky question, not like 'Can we go now?' but more like 'Is a *mandate* the same as a *manifesto*?', a teacher may feel that the student is trying to catch them out. But if we reset our mental compass, moving it away from the point labelled 'Giving my lesson' and towards the lodestar of 'Genuine curiosity', we can learn how our student is attempting to make sense of the lesson. So, as we ourselves become curious and observe and listen to our students carefully to find out how they are thinking, and as we ourselves are open about our own ignorance and show the sources we have to use to check things out, we model behaviour that is valuable in a learning environment. We do not have to be the ones who answer all the questions that students ask. In fact, if students are asking good questions, the chances are strong that we can't answer them all! And students can be encouraged to take responsibility for their own questions. We can write down the question and the name of the student, and gradually help them to answer the question later in the term once they have been exposed to some teaching, reading, thinking and discussion on the topic they expressed curiosity about.

TT3 Finding out what we really do

Maybe, when I look at the list above of recommended behaviours for encouraging thinking, I can be tempted to think, 'Oh! I already do all those.' But if I am honest, I'm not absolutely sure that I *hear* all student contributions, let alone acknowledge them all properly. If I really want to find out what I do in class and to learn what my patterns are, it would be really helpful to invite a colleague in to check this out for me or to sound tape myself and then analyse the tape afterwards.

TT4 Types of teacher questions

We probably ask hundreds of questions in the process of a month's teaching. One way of classifying the questions we ask is by the answers they require. So, for example, we could frame a question to require a brief, specific answer as in:
   'What class of word is *yummy*?' (answer: an adjective).
or to encourage a wide-ranging answer as in:
   'What are some of the things you did last weekend?'

Some people call the narrow-answer questions *closed* or *convergent* and the broad ones *open* or *divergent*. You'll see that although both the questions above start with the word *what*, students can still answer them briefly or at length. So we can say for sure that it is too

Teaching Tips

simple to imagine that questions starting with *what, when, where, who*, etc always prompt brief, narrow, dull, or unthinking responses, or that those starting with *what if, why, how*, or other open questions necessarily lead to wide-ranging, interesting answers. It's the *content* of the question here rather than its form, and the desire of the student to communicate an answer, that together constitute the key to stimulating thinking.

However, it's pretty clear that lots of narrow questions (whatever word they start with) will elicit lots of short answers and so may require less thought on the students' part. We could also check that our questions encourage students not just to recall or to answer questions simply by checking quickly in their course materials, but also to manipulate information, analyse, create and evaluate (see Morgan and Saxton, 2002).

TT5 Answering our own questions

Teachers who are inexperienced and shy of silences or who are really keen to get through lots of material will ask several questions, one after the other, and after waiting just a couple of seconds will answer the question(s) themselves! Once students get used to this and realise that they are not really expected to attempt an answer, and certainly don't have time to think of one, they may well switch off. No thinking necessary there! This will mean that a passive, non-thinking atmosphere will build in the classroom, which will be extremely difficult for teachers to lift.

TT6 Wait-time

Wait-time is when the teacher pauses in class and .... waits!

There are two different times when it is invaluable. First, just after we have asked a question. Secondly, after we have received an answer. Thus ...
    Teacher: What do you notice about the sentences in this story?
    Pause
    Student 1: They're all short.
    Pause
    Student 2: There're no commas or anything.

If we wait after we have asked a question and after a student has ventured an answer, we give students time to think. Research tells us (Rowe, 1978) that good wait-time will get us more and longer answers from more students who will also start to build on each other's contributions. Increasing wait-time also appears to increase student confidence and speculative thinking. It will also give us teachers benefits. The quantity of our questions may go down while the quality may go up. We may become able to ask questions that require our students to do more complex information-processing and thinking. We may thus improve the quality of our own utterances and interventions because we have time to think about them. Disciplinary problems may also decrease. The concept of wait-time can be shared with students too.

If you find pausing after questioning hard, try ...
- noticing your breathing and gestures and keeping them relaxed
- slowly and silently counting 'One Mississippi, two Mississippi ...' up to five, slowly
- calmly looking round the classroom
- mentally checking that your own question was a well-worded, clear and relevant one.

TT7 Echoing

Echoing is when a teacher repeats what a student has just said. Here's an example.
Teacher: 'What do people do to prepare for a job interview?'
Student: 'Wear a suit ...'
Teacher: 'Wear a suit.'

Echoing is a really hard habit to break. If we are even aware that we do it, we usually imagine that we are doing it for all sorts of good reasons, such as to confirm to a student that their answer is a good one, to repeat it loudly enough for others to hear or to model pronunciation. But in fact echoing increases teacher talking time, hands control of the conversation back to the teacher, discourages students from bothering to speak up and supplants praise or encouragement. It's very unnatural in ordinary conversation and hardly encourages thinking!

If we realise we have got into a real habit of echoing, what can we do? Well, we can ask a quiet student to say what they just said a little louder or ask a nearby student to repeat what was said more loudly. Or we can acknowledge the student's contribution, and respond to it flexibly and with real interest, in a naturally communicative way such as by saying, 'Yes, sometimes people buy a new one even!' in the example about the job interview above or – yes, you guessed it! – we can practise using wait-time.

TT8 Follow-up questions

Unlike teacher echoing, follow-up questions can really move thinking on. They are encouraging prompts that help a class to fill out answers that are not quite right or not full enough. They can involve us making encouraging noises, rephrasing the original question, or making it simpler, or can involve briefly reviewing previous information for students to help them recall it.

Brown and Wragg (1993) have suggested that follow-up questions be asked in a gentle way or so that a task is seen as a fun or interesting challenge. Here are some examples.
- 'Mmm, interesting! Can you say more?'
- 'Can anyone give me an example of that?'
- 'Can you tell me the difference between those two?'
- 'Is there another possible reason?'
- 'Now, remember what we said yesterday about …? How does that fit with …?'

Linking back to previous contributions is good follow-up, too, as in …
- 'What did Sari just say?'
- 'Good … so Maria said it means starting a new topic. Juan said it's informal. So now what does it have in common with …?'

This encourages students to listen to each other and validates previous contributions.

What I am suggesting, then, is that we encourage our students to ask questions and that we respond to them well, notice the kinds of question we ourselves ask, make sure we ask a variety with plenty of open-ended ones, lengthen our wait-time, use it in two different places and use skilful follow-up questions and links. Checking these everyday classroom behaviours is pivotal to helping students to understand, think and contribute, and it is pivotal, too, to preventing ourselves from engaging in over-routinised, non-thinking behaviour.

TT9 Roadblocks to communication

The strategies above are not just useful for encouraging students to contribute more and more often when they are concentrating well in a lesson. They are also essential in communicating with students when they are upset or distressed about something. The skill of silence or wait-time, the use of acknowledging responses (like 'Hmm Hmm', 'I see'), good follow-up questions (like 'That's interesting; want to go

Teaching Tips

on?') and 'active listening' (responding to the student's real message) can, according to Thomas Gordon (2003), be learned. He mentions twelve roadblocks to communication in his teacher effectiveness training books and programmes. Gordon explains that he uses the term *roadblocks* to mean our typical and unhelpful responses to students experiencing a problem in life, either inside or outside the class or institution. Roadblocks tend to stop productive, helpful communication.

Gordon sees the twelve roadblocks to communication as being divided into five types. In the first type are these:
1. Ordering, commanding, directing.
   'Stop grumbling and get back to work.'
2. Warning, threatening.
   'You had better get yourself sorted out if you expect to pass the exam.'
3. Moralizing, preaching, using *should* and *ought*.
   'You should leave your personal problems outside the classroom.'
4. Advising, offering solutions or suggestions.
   Example: 'I think you need to get an alarm clock so you can get up on time.'
5. Teaching, lecturing, giving logical arguments.
   'You'd better remember you only have four days to complete that essay.'

The next responses to students tend to communicate a judgemental attitude and imply put-downs:
6. Judging, criticizing, disagreeing, blaming.
   'You are lazy or else a procrastinator.'
7. Name-calling, stereotyping, labelling.
   'Act your age. You are not a small child any more.'
8. Interpreting, analyzing, diagnosing.
   'You are just trying to get out of doing this assignment because you missed the directions due to talking.'

The next two messages try to make the student feel better or to deny there is a problem:
9. Praising, agreeing, giving positive evaluations.

'You are a very competent young woman. I am sure you can figure out a way to finish this assignment.'
10. Reassuring, sympathizing, consoling, supporting.
'I know exactly how you are feeling. If you just get started, it won't seem so bad.'

The next response tries to get more information and to solve the problem for the student:
11. Questioning, probing, interrogating, cross-examining.
'Why did you wait so long to ask for help? How many hours have you put in so far?'

The last type of message tends to change the subject, divert the student or attempt to avoid the whole problem:
12. Withdrawing, distracting, being sarcastic, humouring, diverting.
'Who got up on the wrong side of the bed today?' 'Let's get back to the topic.'

All these ways of responding to students when they are experiencing a problem of some kind convey, according to Gordon, 'unacceptance' messages. I have to confess that on reading them through I realised that I use 4, 9 and 10. I suppose that recognising that I do this is the first step to doing something about it!

If we want our students to think and learn, and if we want to think clearly ourselves and teach, we need to gain skill in building good relationships and good communication with our students. Without these skills, everyone in the room can become bored, turned off or resistant. With them, everyone can feel accepted and can do their best.

TT10 Being positive

It's a very good idea to congratulate students for any non-language-related skills they have, e.g. drawing good stick figures, picking up the tune of a song quickly, being observant enough to spot mistakes on the board, being good at counting games (see activity 1.3), cleaning the board swiftly and well, knowing general knowledge type things. We can do this by thanking them, complimenting them on their contributions or referring to them sincerely as the 'computer expert' etc.

We can also accentuate the positive in their language learning and production by overtly noticing all the things they get right in a text (tick all the correct words, phrases or sentences) or in a classroom utterance ('Great! You got most of that right! Can you just think about the word you used before *the restaurant*?'). We can encourage students to stay realistic about their language learning (see the ideas in activities 1.6 and 1.7) and help them to feel, e.g., 'I don't understand this yet, *but at some point I will!*'

In activity 1.8, there is another nice idea for charging the classroom with positive feelings.

TT11 Getting the target language into the room

No matter how you start your lesson – whether with a warm-up, a cool-down, an advance organiser or a thinking puzzle – it's a good idea to have your students speaking as much of the target language as possible even at elementary level. It would be good if they started thinking straight away in English rather than always going through their mother tongue first. So, in activities 1.13 and 1.14 there are some ideas for getting the target language into the room early on.

TT12 Class routines

Routines are very important in classes. They give a feeling of structure, security and rhythm. We all have them. We have to attract students' attention, for example. We need to mark the transitions between lesson phases. We can do the routine the same way each time or we can vary the way we do it. So, for example, when attracting attention we can sometimes tap on the board and at other times switch the lights on and off quickly, or ring a little bell, shake a tambourine or play a note or two on a penny whistle. A student who is really tall can be asked to stand up and whistle. Try anything rather than lose your voice and your cool by shouting!

In activity 1.15 are some thoughts on another routine that we already have but could inject a little more thought into.

TT13 Moving students around

Talking of routines, students do often seem to get into a habit of sitting in the same place near the same people each lesson. This means they get used to working with, and hearing the voice and ideas of, the same few people near them, so it is a good idea to ask them to move around sometimes. You can do this in many different ways. Here are a few.
- Work out where you want students to sit, and place name cards on the appropriate desks, rather like at a posh dinner party.
- Work out who you want to sit with whom. Then hand out materials for a matching activity, e.g. first halves and second halves of sentences, being careful to give the matching halves to those you wish to pair up. Students then have to mingle to find their other half. Students with matching halves then sit together

Teaching Tips

and make a new start or a new finish to the sentence they have matched.
- Choose a non-threatening, perhaps even silly, aspect of clothing or behaviour. Check quickly if it is likely to give you the even numbers you need for the pairs, trios or quartets that you want, and say, e.g., 'All those wearing brown shoes on this side, all wearing black on that', (or glasses wearers and non, toothpaste tube squeezers versus rollers, cat lovers versus dog lovers, etc).
- Ask students to move around so they are sitting with someone that they have not worked with much before.

TT14 While you are busy

There will be times when you are, for example, writing on the board, sorting out a DVD player, or checking something in a dictionary. Students may lapse into doldrums or mother tongue or silly behaviour at these moments because it may feel to them like a little time off, especially if your back is turned or you are looking away from them. There are lots of things you can ask students to do while you are working that can mean their time is valuably used, e.g. when you are at the board you can:
- ask students to guess what word you are about to write up from seeing the first letter, or ...
- every few words and when you can, tell them what word you are going to write and ask them to spell the word out loud before you write it, or to pronounce it correctly once you have, or ...
- tell them that you will ask them in a minute to state where the stress-marking on what you are writing up should go (or to tell you the word class, or to think of a sentence using one of the words). They should be getting ready for this task while you are writing.

Or while having trouble with a piece of equipment, ask students to think up a test question that they would like to put to their neighbour in a minute. The neighbour can choose to have an easy, difficult or 'demon' question.

TT15 Finishing lessons off

It feels good if we can finish our lesson in a neat and appealing way. Apart from taking the last few minutes to write the class homework on the board, what can we do to finish a class well? We can look forward at the start of class to the work we are about to undertake. We can also provide time and tasks at the end of a lesson to help students consider the work that has been done in class, as in activities 1.16, 1.17. 1.18 and 1.19.

The ways of working discussed in this chapter have slight implications for lesson planning. These are discussed in chapter 3.

1.1 Invent a handshake

> Wake-up idea

Focus: Seeing how inventive people can be. Physical activity. Fun. Vocabulary of movement verbs (see below).

Level: Elementary upwards

Time: 10 minutes

Materials/Preparation: Think up an original gesture of greeting for step 2.

in class

1. Explain that in many countries when people meet for the first time they shake hands. Demonstrate this. When they see each other next time across the street, they may wave. Demonstrate this.

2. Explain that you would like the students to invent a different kind of gesture of greeting, one of their own. It will be unique to them and can be anything that is not rude. It must not be a normal handshake or wave. Demonstrate your own gesture as an example.

3. Encourage students to try out a few different gestures with their faces, arms, shoulders or other parts of their body until they find one they like.

4. If you have room, ask students to stand up, walk around and greet each other in their new ways. If you have limited space, briefly invite one student to greet the class in their own special way from their normal seat. Everybody else should watch carefully and then mirror the gesture back to the student, thus learning the student's gesture and greeting them.

5. Continue by repeating step 4 as often as you have time for.

6. You may be able to teach a few words as you go along (such as *shrug, wiggle, wriggle, blink* etc, if students use these movements).

Follow-up
Next time you meet the students, you can either use one of their own greeting gestures or continue by asking those who were missed out last time to introduce their gesture to the class, who then copy it back to the student.

1.2 Simply stimulate

> Wake-up idea

Focus: Using an unusual, wordless stimulus to get students thinking. Describing a short stimulus and saying what they think about it.

Level: Elementary upwards

Time: 10 minutes

Materials/Preparation: Find an interesting short video on the internet, a trick picture, a short piece of music, a cartoon, a reproduction of a painting or anything interesting that does not have words attached to it (see Note below for suggestions).

in class

1. Tell students this is a fluency exercise so they should not worry about making mistakes.

2. Flash the stimulus to the students or play it once.

3. Ask them to tell their partner briefly in English what they saw or heard, to try to describe it and then to say how they feel about it.

4. In plenary, feed in any useful expressions or vocabulary related to what they saw.

Note
A great source of short, language-free scenes is YouTube (e.g. the 'Hahaha' or 'Charlie bit my finger' videos or Jamie Keddie's video clips at http://lessonstream.org/browse-lessons/.

1.3 Counting games

> Wake-up idea

Focus: Helping individual students to come together, settle and become mentally alert by doing something unusual. Practising numbers in English.

Level: Any

Time: 5–10 minutes

Materials/Preparation: None.

in class

1. Make sure students can count from 1 to 8 (or 1 to 12 or whatever you prefer) out loud.

2. Ask students to count from 1 to 8 out loud several times. The first time they count they should stress the first number so, 'ONE two three four five …' etc.

3. The second time they stress the second number as in 'one TWO three four' etc.

4. Next time, they stress the third number as in 'one two THREE', and so on until the last chant, which should be 'one two three four five six seven EIGHT'.

Follow-up / Variations

A Students can count backwards in the same way from 8 to 1. This is more difficult and requires more thought.

B Students can be asked to count out loud as before. This time, each number has the same stress, but they have to count up and back missing out one number, e.g. the number 3. This would sound like this:

   One two four five six seven eight, eight seven six five four two one.

Once students have got the hang of missing out just one number, they can be asked to miss out more than one number, say 3 and 5, or 7 and 9. It takes concentration!

1.3 Counting games

C Students can be asked to count up and back in little increments like this:

12, 1232, 123432, 12345432, 1234565432, 123456765432, 123456787654321.

This takes a bit of practice, but can be followed by the even trickier exercise where you start from the top as in 87, 8767, 876567, 876545678 etc.

Note
If you are musical, you can use a basic eight-count and do all the above while at the same time singing scales!

Acknowledgement
Thanks to Susan Wanless, conductor of the University of Kent Chorus, for these.

1.4 Expanding a sentence

> Wake-up idea

Focus: Helping individual students to settle down and become mentally alert. Learning about English syntax.

Level: Elementary upwards

Time: 10-15 minutes

Materials/Preparation: Prepare a short starter sentence (for step 1).

in class

1. Write a very short sentence on the board, e.g. *I love exercise* or *I have a cat*.

2. Give the students, say, three minutes to expand the sentence by five or seven or ten or more words depending on their level and the amount of time you have. The sentences students make don't have to be true. They should be written down.
A student adding fourteen words might thus write, 'My mum and I have now got a new, black, girl cat and we love her very much.'

3. Ask students to read out their sentences. You can react naturally to what they have written and can give gold stars for the longest, most interesting, funniest, or strangest sentence.

Follow-up / Variations
The exercise can be reversed, i.e., you can write a very long sentence on the board. Here is an example: 'The thing I like most about my wonderful job as a teacher of form 2A is not that the students are great, although this is of course true, but the fact that I can work with them in Room 15 and so get a fabulous view of the beech tree in the garden.' Ask students to shorten your sentence by six to ten words whilst still writing a grammatical sentence. Again, the sentence doesn't have to be true.

Acknowledgement
I learned this from Ann Swarbrick.

1.5 Clem's spiral (and other one-minute activities)

Calming-down idea

Focus: Helping individual students to settle down and to start to focus. Developing hand-eye co-ordination and a sense of timing.

Level: Any

Time: 5 minutes

Materials/Preparation: None.

in class

1. Ask students to get a large sheet of paper (A4) and a pencil or pen.

2. Explain that when you say 'Go!' they should place the tips of their pens somewhere near the outside of the paper and start to draw a spiral, moving slowly inwards as they draw it until they come to the middle. They must not lift their pen off the paper until they have finished. They also have to judge how long a minute is and get to the centre and stop at exactly 60 seconds from when you say 'Go!'

3. Say, 'Go!' Watch as all the heads go down and supreme silence and concentration descend. Time the minute. Tell the students when it is up and comment on who was a speed queen or a hare and who was a relaxed chap or a tortoise.

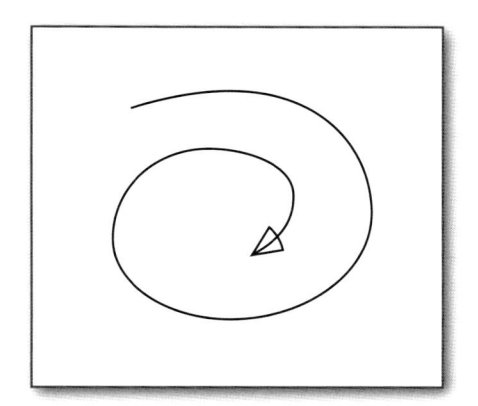

CHAPTER 1: FUNDAMENTALS

1.5 Clem's spiral (and other one-minute activities)

Follow-up / Variations
A Do this to music, e.g. to a recording of the *Minute Waltz*.

B Students use the idea of judging how long a minute is while doing other things than drawing spirals, for example while walking from one end of the classroom to the other, while unscrambling an anagram (which is good for vocabulary review and spelling), while going to their favourite place in their mind's eye or while watching their in and out breaths and noticing what sorts of thoughts wander in and out of their minds while they are doing so.

Notes
The whole point of this exercise is that the class is communally quiet and thinking about something reasonably peaceful for a whole minute.
An awareness of time can be useful if your students need to estimate how long things take, for example in meeting deadlines.

Acknowledgement
I learned this from Cranmer and Laroy (1992) p. 10.

1.6 The learning dip and rise

> Helping students be realistic about language learning

Focus: Helping students to understand that learning a new language takes time and that they will need to be patient with themselves as they gradually learn more.

Level: Any

Time: 15-20 minutes the first time, then 5-10 minutes subsequently

Materials/Preparation: Think of something that you are currently learning (for step 1). Optional, prepare a diagram (see below).

in class

1. Introduce the topic of learning and give an example of something you are learning yourself. This could be how to put music onto your iPod or how to make a pottery plate, do a yoga exercise, or understand a difficult book. It needs to be a real example. Tell your class briefly how you felt at the start (enthusiastic? daunted?), how you have had some successes (that made you feel good?) and some difficult times when you couldn't understand or do something (that made you feel fed up?).

2. If you like, show them a diagram of a dip and a rise.

Enthusiasm!
Excitement!
Confusion
Understanding

3. Using whatever terms you feel best suit your students, label parts of the experience or the diagram as you talk it through. You could use words such *excitement* or *enthusiasm* for the beginning phase. Then, add words such as *clarity* and *understanding* for the good parts of the experience. For harder phases use *confusion* and so on.

1.6 The learning dip and rise

4. Once you have talked through one experience using the figure, identify other examples from your own life and theirs. Then switch to the idea of learning a new word in English. Tell the students how many things there are to know about a word (e.g. pronunciation of individual sounds, stress, spelling, hyphenation, meaning, associations, word class, what it doesn't mean, collocation).

Explain that we need to meet a new word many times within a certain period of time to learn all these things and then to be able to hear the word, say it, read it and write it fast, appropriately and at will. Sometimes, just when you think you have learned something, you realise there is yet more to learn. You can relate this idea to the 'dip and rise' figure so that students can see that even with one single word we can feel up at some times and downhearted at others! Use any metaphor or analogy that you feel will help students further, e.g. tell the students that together you will all be building the language like a house and so it will take time.

Follow-up
Refer to this experience or figure or analogy whenever you feel things are getting tough for learners.

Encourage students to tackle times of dip or plateau in their learning. You can do this by teaching them the following meta-cognitive questions and by working with them on answering them:
- What did I do last time I hit this problem?
- What resources are there to help me?
- What IS the problem? How can I break it down?
- Can I then work on bits of the problem?
- What can I learn from other people to help me?
- What do I believe and what am I feeling about this? Do these beliefs and feelings help me?
- How can I think BIG now?

Acknowledgement
I first saw this sort of dip and rise visual on the Philosophy for Children web site at: www.p4c.com. And a good illustration of the 'roller coaster of your language learning' is given in Murphey, T., *Language Hungry!* (2006), p 9.

1.7 My favourite mistakes

> Helping students be realistic about language learning

Focus: Helping students to understand that making mistakes is something everybody does and that it is useful, as it can help us to improve. Injecting humour into correction. Helping students notice their own mistakes.

Level: Any

Time: 10–15 minutes the first time; 5–10 minutes subsequently

Materials/Preparation: Make a note of mistakes that students often make in their utterances in class and in their written work in class or in homework. If you teach monolingual classes, some mistakes will be made by many or most students. If you teach multilingual students, the mistakes will often be different from student to student.
Select the most important or common mistakes and write them up on the board in sentences that are very close to ones students have actually produced. Don't write up *exactly* what they have produced, as you want to protect any one student or students from feeling shown up or picked on.

in class

1. Ask students to consider, alone or in pairs or trios, what is wrong with each sentence on the board and how it can be corrected. (At higher levels include some sentences that are perfectly acceptable and warn students that you have done so.)

2. Once the sentences have been discussed and corrected, ask students to make a separate section in their notebooks entitled *My Favourite Mistakes*. They are to write down both the incorrect and the corrected versions of any of the sentences previously discussed that they feel they are guilty of! The incorrect ones should include some glaring visual reminder of incorrectness, such as a red cross, through the appropriate part.

Follow-up

A Refer to this section of their notebooks often. When correcting utterances in class, say to a student humorously 'Ah! I think that is one of your favourite mistakes!' and wait for them to correct it by, if necessary, checking it in their notebooks. Don't correct it for them. They can now be independent in this matter.

1.7 My favourite mistakes

B   When correcting homework, you can write 'FM!' and a smiley ☺ next to any common, previously discussed mistake. And then ask the student to correct it themselves.

1.8 Just one good thing

> Charging the classroom with positive feelings

Focus: Introducing a positive atmosphere. Use of Past Simple and Present Perfect tenses in personal statements.

Level: Elementary upwards

Time: Depends on the number of students who would like to say something

Materials/Preparation: Think of one or two examples of things that have gone right for you (for steps 1 and 4)

in class

1. Ask students to think back over the morning (or evening or day or week) so far, and to think of just one simple thing that has gone right or that is positive for them. Tell them it doesn't have to be a big thing. It can be something as simple as a cool glass of orange juice, or a friendly text message from a friend, or that the weather is a bit warmer than of late. You can give your own simple example, if you like. Then ask for other offerings.

2. Practise your wait-time! (See TT6.)

3. Ask if anybody is ready to offer something. Not everybody has to speak. If someone does, listen well to what they say and thank them. Then practise your wait-time again.

4. Once some people have spoken and if you feel things have slowed down a bit say, 'Okay … any last contributions?' and wait again. This usually brings a few more! You could pop another contribution in here too.

5. When you really feel that everyone who wants to speak has spoken, ask, 'Is everyone ready to move on?' If they are, do so.

1.9 'Menu' on the board

> Seeing where we are going

Focus: Looking forward to the contents of a lesson. The language of plans.

Level: Any

Time: 2–3 minutes.

Materials/Preparation: You need to know what you plan to do in a particular module and be prepared to write this up on the board before you start teaching (see below).
Each lesson, keep one part of your board, say a column down the left-hand side, for a list of topics that will come up in the lesson. You can have fun with a menu theme by dividing that column into sections headed *Starter, Main course, Side dishes, Dessert or Coffee* and *Take-home doggy bag*, and writing the topics up in the various sections.

in class

1. Point to the menu and briefly read it through. Students may want to ask you questions about items on the menu. You can then explain what they are, why they are important, etc. You may want to use time connectors such as, *first, then, next, later on* and language of planning such as *We're going to ... if we have time.*

2. Then leave the menu on the board and proceed with the lesson.

Follow-up
At the end of the lesson you can refer back to the menu notes on the board to ask students what has been covered and to point out anything you did not have time to work on.

Variations
A Once students have got used to the idea of looking ahead to the contents of the lesson and have learned the vocabulary of meal courses, you can switch the metaphor to another one, such as a business meeting (*agenda, apologies, minutes of the last meeting, points for discussion, AOB*) or a sports match (from hockey: *bully-off, first half, refreshments, second half, extra time, final whistle*) depending on the interests of the group.

1.9 'Menu' on the board

B Instead of using a theme like *menus* or *meeting agendas*, you can instead write up the headings *What?*, *Why?* and *How?* on the board so that you can share with students your goals and purposes, and the strategies that you are going to help them to use; see activity 1.18.

C Students can be encouraged to set their own goals too. These can be individual ones, group ones or ones in response to an external goal such as sitting and passing a public exam.

1.10 Concept map ... a true advance organiser

> Seeing where we are going

Focus: Students look forward to what they are about to do in the lesson and see how it fits in with a larger scheme of work.

Level: Elementary upwards

Time: 10 minutes the first time, 5 minutes subsequently, over several lessons

Materials/Preparation: Using a board, handout or other display device, build a concept map to show an overview of the work coming up. Let's imagine you have a writing class and you want to help students understand and use paragraphs successfully. You could use the visual below.

PARAGRAPHS

- What they look like
- What they are for
- What they contain
- What they don't contain

Under "What they contain": Topic sentence, Supporting sentences, Lexical variation

Under "What they don't contain": Irrelevant sentences

in class

1. Take one or more parts of the diagram and elicit what students already know about it/them.

2. Show your students examples of topic, supporting and irrelevant sentences and lexical variation, so that they know what they are, and give them writing tasks to practise generating them, e.g. unjumbling sentences, finding topic sentences and picking out irrelevant sentences.

3. As the learning points under each part of the concept map (see illustration) are met and understood, students can add them to their notebooks under the bubbles of the concept map. Thus, for example, under the bubble *What they look like*, students can write:
    - First line indented

1.10 Concept map ... a true advance organiser

- Write to end of lines
- Hyphenate long words at the end of the lines
- Last sentence can finish anywhere on the line
- Not too short
- Not too long.

Students are thus working on the concept map from the more general heading to do with paragraph appearance to the more specific points of what it is that a paragraph's appearance consists of. In this way they can learn what paragraphing is and how it works.

Follow-up
If, later on, students notice something about the topic you have been working on, e.g. in this instance, that in fact first lines of paragraphs are often not indented in typed documents, they can add a question mark to that first point on their concept map.

Acknowledgement
A concept map is an example of an Advance Organiser. The idea of Advance Organisers is attributed to cognitive psychologist David Ausubel (1968). Advance Organisers are devices teachers can use when introducing a new topic to enable learners to orient themselves to what is coming. They help a learner relate new learning to what is already known. They thus need to be at a higher level of abstraction than the immediate lesson content. They can also involve discussion of what will follow later once the ideas and concepts currently being presented have been understood.

1.11 Crazy questions *or* 'Thunks'

> Starting to think up ideas

Focus: To wake students up and get them thinking, talking and rationalising in a non-judgemental manner, to encourage students to look at things in unusual ways. Speaking and listening.

Level: Pre-Intermediate upwards

Time: 10 minutes on a regular basis

Materials/Preparation: Select one question you think will amuse or surprise students (see variations and acknowledgement for ideas and sources).

in class

1. At the start of a lesson, explain to students that you are going to ask them an unusual question. They need to think of an answer to the question. They do not have to write anything in their notebooks. They should not shout the idea out but simply hold it in their minds. Tell them that there is no *one* right answer and there are no wrong answers. But they do have to justify their answer and say why they think it is a good one.

2. Ask an unusual question, e.g. 'What colour is Friday?' (or the day you happen to be in the classroom with them). Repeat the question only once and wait for a few minutes while students think.

3. Invite students to put up their hands. Select one and let them give you an answer.

4. Accept the answer as the truth, e.g. 'I see. So, Friday is green. Thanks. Can you tell me why it is, please?' Wait for the justification, which might be anything from 'I play hockey on Friday and the grass is green' to 'Green means *Go* and I can go home for the weekend'. As long as the reason is somehow connected to the topic, accept it.

5. Keep waiting, listening and accepting the answers and the rationales. Enjoy them. If they are funny or unusual, let your face show this. You don't need to judge their results or comment on whether they were really thinking well at this stage. This is a fun, warm-up exercise and just designed to get an encouraging atmosphere going.

1.11 Crazy questions or 'Thunks'

Variations
At the start of lessons, on different days, or whenever you want to pull students together, wake them up and get them thinking, you can use this idea. Other questions you can use are: 'If horses ruled the world, what changes would we see?' 'What does a food mixer and this class have in common?' 'How could you improve a teddy bear so that it is more fun to play with?', 'How would life be different if we had eyes in the back of our head as well as in the front?' See Gilbert below for many, many others.

Acknowledgement
I got the name for this idea and lots of great questions from Ian Gilbert (2007).

1.12 Puzzles

> Starting to think up ideas

Focus: Getting students thinking at the start of a class.

Level: Depends on the puzzle

Time: Depends on the puzzle

Materials/Preparation: There are many different kinds of puzzles that we can use with students for a few minutes at the start of class; see below for ideas.

in class

1. Give out a puzzle and give students a time limit in which to think about it alone first. Then ask them to compare notes in pairs.

2. When the time is up, ask people to comment on the puzzle in plenary. This set of steps is often called 'Think, pair, share' and is used in Co-operative Learning. It was developed by Lyman (1981).

Example puzzles you can give your students
- Guess from any notes left behind on the board (naughty last teacher!) what the last lesson in the room was about.
- Work in pairs to complete the spelling of words from previous lessons which are written with letters missing on the board or on slips of paper.
- Decide which words or phrases go together from an array of broken collocations on the board.
- Decide what comes next in unfinished lists of items that go from small to large, e.g. *hamlet, village, town* ... or from specific to general, e.g. *dog, pet, animal* ... or general to specific, e.g. *living thing, plant, evergreen* ...
- Put disorganised items into an order, e.g. *Venus, Mercury, Earth, Mars* ... or *trains, bikes, wheels, carts* ...
- Match or make up captions to cartoons.
- Draw or describe pictures that fit made-up titles for paintings.
- See where pictures differ from the texts that describe them inaccurately.
- Find (or write) the second half of jumbled two-line jokes or of conditional sentences.
- Read through a list of their own utterances written up on the board, and decide in pairs which ones are right or wrong and how the wrong ones should be corrected.
- Do simple jigsaw puzzles that show useful pictures, e.g. a map of their or another part of the world or a photo of the school garden, before describing the whole.

1.12 Puzzles

You can also do the following:
- Ask a problematic question, such as 'What if colours changed without warning and red became green and green became red – what problems would there be and how could we solve them?'
- Draw two differing stress profiles on the board – e.g. ■ ■ (for words that are pronounced like *blackboard*) and ■ ■ ■ (for words pronounced like *family*) – then ask students to come up with, say, ten words that have the same stress patterns.
- Ask questions about things that people don't usually notice, such as 'How many letters of the English alphabet, in CAPITAL form, have curves, and how many have only straight lines? (Key: BCDGJOPQRSU=11 and AEFHIKLMNTVWXYZ=15)
- Give students some general knowledge questions to answer.
- Tell just the first half of a story, promising to tell the last half at the end of the lesson if students make some good predictions about what might happen next.

Notes
As we know, there are many other kinds of puzzles including: themed or non-themed anagrams, acrostics, spot the difference pictures, word search, sudoku, jumbled pictures, jigsaws, logic problems, general knowledge quizzes, matching or odd one out exercises, simple, themed or cryptic crosswords, 'what connects these words?' quizzes, relationships between words puzzles, number sequence puzzles.

We just need to make sure that the ratio of quiet, individual, puzzle-solving time and student time spent talking about what they are doing, what they have done and what can be done with the result, is weighted towards using English.

You can make your own vocabulary review puzzles such as crosswords, word searches etc at www.puzzlemaker.com.

1.13 Labelling the room

> Thinking in English

Focus: Helping students to think in the target language without mentally translating into mother tongue. Room and furniture vocabulary.

Level: Any

Time: 5–10 minutes per class on a regular basis

Materials/Preparation: Sticky labels or slips of paper or pictures (see step 1).

in class

1. At lower levels, pick a few ordinary classroom objects/nouns such as *desk*, *window*, *board* and teach them to your students in your usual way. When you want to review this vocabulary, give students sticky labels or post-it notes and invite them to stick or place these onto the objects. If this is not possible in your setting because you share your room with a teacher of a different language or you are not allowed to use the furniture in this way, then make a drawing or ask students who are good at drawing to make one. Older students may find it fun to cut out pictures from magazines. Alternatively you can find a magazine picture and cut it out and copy it. Each student can then label their copy of the picture.

2. Slowly build up the room vocabulary concentrating, at lower levels, on nouns like *door*, *bin*, *chair*, *pencil case* etc. After they have a good number of words mostly learned, you can take all the existing labels off and keep them. Then have a review slot later on, when students tell you where to place those labels back onto the objects or onto a visual for review. Alternatively, keep the old labels for variation A below

Follow-up
Once the room is done, you can move on to new topics such as *classmate's clothing*, or the details of a chair (e.g. *back*, *seat*, *rungs*, *cushion* and so on)

Variations
A At higher levels, review the simple nouns (e.g. *wall* and *light*), but then encourage students to write onto the existing label, or to make a new label with an adjective, e.g. *white wall* or *electric light*; you can build from *wall* to *white wall* to *plain white wall with marks on it* etc.

1.13 Labelling the room

B Students can draw or take pictures of their rooms at home and label the pictures. Then, once you have checked the words are correct, they can write out labels and stick or place them onto the real objects in their real rooms. They can also choose favourite objects connected to their hobbies (e.g. *tennis racket*, *guitar*) or family life (e.g. *my cat*) and draw pictures of these or take photos of them and label these, with your help.

Note
All the following can help with the production of images:
clip art, internet images (remember to check for any copyright restrictions), digital cameras, picture dictionaries. The website www.onelook.com can help with the words.

1.14 Grammarless beginnings

> Thinking in English

Focus: Helping students to start thinking and communicating with others in English in classroom situations even when they don't have a high level of English.

Level: Beginner–Elementary

Time: 15 minutes a lesson on a regular basis

Materials/Preparation: Selection of a topic and connected phrases (see below).

in class

1. Encourage students to greet each other in English at the start of class, by teaching them a very simple dialogue such as one of those below.

   To reinforce names:
   > A: You're?
   > B: Gerhard!
   > A: Ah yes, Gerhard!

   To ask about health:
   > A: OK?
   > B: Yes! You?
   > A Yes, thanks!

2. Teach the dialogue, practise it with the correct stress and intonation, and then insist on students using it at the start of class. Once students can do this easily, build in a little variety e.g.:

   > A: OK?
   > B: No! Not OK!
   > A: Oh, pity!

3. Teach more of these short, grammarless dialogues, ones which are useful for other times of the lesson. Here are some examples:

   Before a weekend:
   > A: Nice weekend!
   > B: Thanks! You too!

1.14 Grammarless beginnings

After a weekend:
> A: Good weekend?
> B: Yes! You?
> A: Not bad!

Before a break:
> Teacher: Break?
> Students: Break!

After explaining something:
> Teacher: Got it? (*or* OK? *or* All right?)
> Students: Got it! (*or* OK! *or* All right!)

Or:
> Teacher: Got it?
> Students: No!

Or:
> Teacher; Stuck?
> Students: Yes!

Before pair work:
> A: You start!
> B: No! You start!
> A: Oh, OK!

Discussing opinions:
> A; I think … And you?
> B: Me too. (*or* No, I think …)

After pair work:
> A: Finished?
> B: Mmm … think so!

1.14 Grammarless beginnings

After any work:

> A: Nice working with you! (*or* talking to you, seeing you, chatting to you)
> B: Nice working with you too! (*or* talking to you too, seeing you too, chatting to you too)

Borrowing something:

> A: Got a pen?
> B: Here!
> A: Ta!

Before moving on:

> Teacher: Ready? (*or* OK?)
> Students: Ready! (*or* OK!)

Follow-up
Ask students to write these little dialogues in a special part of their notebooks. Teach them just like any other bits of target language and insist on them being used in class at appropriate times. You can encourage the use of the language by asking students to write a couple of these gambits on slips of coloured paper. They try to say the words or phrases some time in the lesson. As they do, they lay their coloured slip down on the edge of their desk. If they haven't managed to use the phrase by the end of the lesson, they keep the slip of coloured paper and try to get rid of it next time.

(See also 'Taking the register', activity 1.15.)

Note
The most important thing about these dialogues is that they are in natural spoken English and contain very few auxiliary verbs or other tricky bits of grammar, so they get very low-level students started.

1.15 Taking the register

> Using a class routine to get more English into the classroom

Focus: Turning a necessary but often mindless routine into an interesting exercise that encourages students to concentrate and answer rapidly in English in various ways.

Level: Beginner upwards

Time: 5 minutes

Materials/Preparation: Select a number of very short, grammarless opening gambits (see 'Grammarless beginnings', activity 1.14). If necessary, have these gambits written on a list near you so that you don't have to commit them to memory and can produce them fast.

in class

1. When you take the register, start from a different place in the list each time and, depending on the number of students you have, pause after every fifth or sixth or seventh student's name so that different students are addressed each time.

2. Say something in English to the individual students you call on. Wait for an answer, also in English. So the roll call might sound something like this:

> T: Maria. OK?
> S: OK!

> T: All right, Jean?
> S: All right!

> T: Gol, nice weekend?
> S: Nice weekend!

> T; Ready, Kumiko?
> S: Ready!

1.15 Taking the register

Follow-up
As students learn more grammarless conversations these can be woven in so that students are choosing between different possible responses rather than, as at first, simply copying what the teacher says, but with a change in intonation.

Variations
You can use calling the roll to practise all kinds of different things, e.g.:

Prepositions of place: 'Who is the student sitting between / behind / next to / near / in front of / opposite X?' Class says 'Liz!'

Descriptions of people or clothing: 'What's the name of the student wearing a red sweater and blue hair slide?' Class says 'Jean!'

Present Continuous and Present Simple for absentees: 'What do you suppose Eli is doing right now? Sleeping? Does she usually sleep in?'

Students can take over the role of 'register person' too by trying out any of the ideas above.

1.16 Solo silent reflection

> Ending a lesson well

Focus: Encouraging students to look back to see what they have learned in a lesson.

Level: Elementary upwards

Time: 5–10 minutes

Materials/Preparation: None.

in class

1. Give a task that encourages private thinking by asking students questions such as these:

   - 'Think back over what we have done in the last half hour and prepare one comment and one question on it. You have four minutes to do this.'
   - 'Sort the new words and phrases on the board according to theme or register or word class, or ones you think you will remember and ones you think you will forget.'
   - 'Write down the words you have learned in this lesson and then consider the question *How do I know that I know these words?*' Students may come up with answers here such as 'Can I say the word, spell it, translate it and use it in a sentence?' (see Jones and Swarbrick 2004, p. 55).
   - 'Write down two actions you will take as a result of today's lesson.'
   - 'Write down the last learning point in your own words in your learning log notebook.'

Note
Some people can think well in public, and enjoy listening to other people and bouncing ideas around with them. The intensely social atmosphere of a normal EFL class does not suit everyone, however. Some students need quiet time to organise their thoughts. So, it can be important to build quiet time in at the end of class.

1.17 Keyword group mapping

> Ending a lesson well

Focus: Encouraging students to look back to see what they have learned.

Level: Elementary upwards

Time: 15 minutes

Materials/Preparation: Make sure you remember in detail what work you have done in a specific lesson or module.

in class

1. Ask students to think back on the lesson they have just experienced and pick out or think up three key words or phrases that represent something important for them in the learning. They should write these down.

2. Once they have had time to do so, if you have a small class ask each student round the class to read one out loud. If a student says something interesting, other students can add it to their lists or ask questions about it. If you have a large class, ask students to do this in groups of four.

3. As students read out different things, this will jog the memories of other students and will also show you what they found memorable in the lesson.

4. If you notice they have missed out some of the learning points, you can reflect on why this might be and make a mental note to come back to the topics.

1.18 What? How? Why?

> Ending a lesson well

Focus: Encouraging students to look back to see what they have learned in a lesson, how and why.

Level: Elementary upwards

Time: 5 minutes

Materials/Preparation: Make sure you remember in detail **what** work you have done in a specific lesson or module, **how** it was done and **why**.

in class

1. Draw three columns on the board, labelled:

   What?   *How?*   *Why?*

2. For each part of the lesson, elicit from students what the learning point was, how it was dealt with and why it is important. Write this up, e.g.:

What?	*How?*	*Why?*
Past Simple; Regular and irregular verbs; Questions, statements and negatives	Teacher's funny story about holiday, and our questions	So we can ask people about recent events

Follow-up / Variations
Instead of the *what, how, why* column headings above, you can use different ways of reflecting on work:

A Today we looked at ... and ...
   In what ways are these the same / In what ways are they different?

B Which of these did we do today? How did we use them?
   You can then show a list of all the things you did, with several that you didn't mixed in. (The list of 'things we did' can be of classroom groupings, e.g. work alone, pair work etc; of skill types, e.g. speaking or writing; or, if you have decided to work overtly on thinking skills and to deal with the metalanguage involved, the list could be of types of thinking, such as brainstorming, categorising, considering, comparing etc.)

C See also 'Concept sheets', activity 2.3.

1.19 Transfer

> Ending a lesson well

Focus: Endeavouring to make sure that learners see how what they are learning fits into a bigger picture and that learning goes out of the classroom with the student and can be used in other contexts.

Level: Intermediate upwards

Time: 5 minutes

Materials/Preparation: None.

in class

1. Ask students to repeat the ideas, words, grammar points, skills, dialogues or whatever they have been learning that lesson in a different way from the one in which they have just learned it (which was probably while sitting down, near their normal partner, writing in biro or speaking in a normal voice).

   Students can be asked, for example, to:
   - change the pitch of their voice, whisper or sound happy, sad or interested while saying language from the lesson
   - stand up and say it or move around the room saying it
   - imagine they are saying it while waiting for a bus or dancing in a disco, and mime doing these things while they are speaking
   - repeat the lesson language with different partners, or with a different topic.
   - mentally rehearse it without saying it out loud, or write it in big letters or trace it in the air with their fingers or use a green board pen or draw a picture connected with it.

   In short, they are allowed to review the material in any way at all except the way they have learned it.

2. Once students have tried a few of the ideas above, ask them what other different ways of reviewing material they could use, and next time try out some of their ideas.

1.19 Transfer

Follow-up / Variations
Students can be asked how the new material:

A fits with past learning

B could be useful in a science class or a history class

C could help them outside class, outside the institution, in real life

D could be summarised, expanded or added

CHAPTER 2
BUILDING CONCEPTS, LOOKING FOR PATTERNS AND MEMORISING

Teaching Tips

TT1 **Building concepts**

Learning a language is a long process. And the learning does not necessarily come in handy chunks that become crystal clear, one by one, in an accretive way. It is not as if we were making beads and then stringing them together to make a necklace. Instead, we often very slowly build our understanding of individual sounds, words and phrases, verb tenses, and ways of doing things in the target language. We gradually get better at reading and writing different kinds of texts, and expressing what we want to say to different people in different situations over time. We do this by meeting things again and again, by circling round and round them from different angles. We try things out and take risks and make mistakes and then realise even more things. We can't get it all in one hit. As teachers, we can both help students with the gradual building of concepts and also with the patience necessary to bear the waiting and partial understanding and all that revisiting.

Teacher work before broaching a concept in class
Before we can make concepts clear to students, we have to understand the concepts well ourselves. Then we need to consider how we will lay the concept out for students. This may take quite a bit of thinking on our part. Below is a list that we can use to make sure we have thought concepts out well enough to introduce them to our students. In a way, it describes what teaching or mediating learning really involves. It is thus quite long. But we can use different sections of it over time. Apart from my own learning and teaching experience, to compile the checklist I have drawn on Wragg and Brown (1993) and Lidz (2002, in Lin and Mackay 2004).

Checklist

Understanding the topic myself
- Is the topic, whether chosen by me, the students or the course book, relevant, useful and engaging to the students?
- What is the whole topic?
- What is the sub-topic?
- What is the relationship between these two?

Working from the known to the unknown or not!
- If I am planning to work from the known to the unknown, what past activities that are related can I recap on, how much do students already know about the topic and how can I find this out?
- How can students refresh what they have done before on this?
- Is the new part challenging enough but not too daunting for students?
- Whether I am working from the known to the unknown or, instead, plunging off onto

Teaching Tips

something brand new like a magic carpet ride, how can I get students interested in the new content?
- How can I make sure students know what they are learning, why they are learning it and what my intentions are?

Introducing the topic
- How can I draw on their experience and make sure the content, tasks and activities are personally significant to them?
- Are there any new terms I need to introduce?
- What will I introduce first?

Making things clear throughout
- How can I use voice, gesture, pauses, visual and audio aids, real objects, analogies, situations, examples, questions and tasks etc to clarify the concept for students?
- How will I enable students to notice the salient features of the concept such as its sound, sight, meaning and use?
- Is the work I've planned really clear and well-organised?
- Is the language I want to use appropriate to their level?

Taking stock
- How will we summarise every so often?
- How can I alter my pace or level if necessary?
- How can I keep myself out of the way and allow student learning to take place?
- Where is the students' chance to formulate and ask questions, to predict, to clarify, to take risks, to reflect, to speak as themselves, to self-test and to set their own learning goals?

Checking student understanding
- How will I know if students have grasped the concept I had intended they should?
- How can I tell if other useful things have been learned as well?
- How can I praise students and offer specific feedback on what has been done well and what remains to be done?

Reviewing
- How can I encourage students to link the learning explicitly with past, current, parallel and future experiences?
- How can I encourage students to recycle or revise this work?
- How can I revisit this work and test the concept with students?
- Can I help them with their concept sheets? (See activity 2.3.)

You may well want to edit the checklist above so that it reflects things you feel are very important. So, you might like to add, e.g., 'How can I cater for learners with differing intelligences or learning styles?' or 'What outcome or product am I expecting?' or 'How can I use play to open the doors to creativity and imagination?' (Thanks to Margit Szesztay for this last question.)

Teaching Tips

TT2 **Looking for patterns**

Learners need to notice the differences between how things are in their own language and how they are in the target language. A lot has been written on this idea of 'noticing the gap'. A quick review of some points is at http://writing.berkeley.edu/TESL-EJ/ej23/a2.html.

Within the target language itself, students need to notice patterns so that by understanding what needs to stay the same and what needs to change they can use the patterns, almost like templates, to generate plenty of similar examples that express their own meanings. In activity 2.6 are some ways of getting into the whole idea of noticing similarities and differences.

Once you have had fun building the 'noticing patterns' mindset in students, using the activities in activity 2.8, you can segue into the whole business of encouraging them to notice patterns in language too.

If English is your first language or you are extremely at home in it, you may need to re-sensitise yourself to the sorts of patterns that exist within it! There are patterns in the constituent building blocks of individual words (such as prefixes like *re-* and *de-*, and suffixes like *-able*, and in singulars and plurals, and in word class such as nouns, adjectives, adverbs). There are patterns within groups of words or lexical chunks (e.g. *time will tell* or *top tips* or *one week wonder*).We need to remember the patterning influence of grammar too, for our students will certainly notice how things look the same (e.g. *can't*, *won't*, *don't*) and sound the same (e.g. *the dresses and tresses of princesses*). There are frames from which students can produce a large number of useful variants, e.g. 'too + adjective *to* + verb...' (*too tired to run*, or *too poor to buy it*). There are patterns in the normal word order of sentences (Subject +Verb+ Object), and in the indication of what is new or important in discourse. There are patterns in text types, story genres, in conversational gambits. There are patterns, too, in how vague or specific a culture likes to be.

What some students naturally do and others need help with is scan for similarity and difference, and notice what stays the same and what changes in a pattern. When working on visible patterns in language we very often use underlining, tables, capitals, colour and written translations. When dealing with audible patterns we use tapping and clapping and conductor-like hand-waving and gestures. We use phonology charts and diagrams, and chants and rhymes and songs, and forward and back chaining. We can reinforce all these methods with discussion and questions and concept sheets (see activity 2.3). We can get the students themselves using all the above methods too.

TT3 **Memorising**

It is generally thought that we can remember from five to nine small items for about 30 seconds (Miller, 1956). Since I have real trouble remembering dates, times and phone numbers myself, this seems to me to be a pretty optimistic guesstimate!

In language learning we need to remember things that are bigger than this and to remember them for longer. We thus need to build them up into chunks, store them, and then rehearse them at regular intervals. There are many ideas our students can utilise to help them with this important business of continuing to notice things about new language and to memorise it. First, the meeting of the items can be enhanced so it is lively and interesting, and involves several different senses. As mentioned above we can use colour, rhyme, chants, symbols and so on for this. We can group items by semantic sets and otherwise endow them with meaning via situations and stories and with personal significance for students themselves. In activities 2.11 onwards are some ideas for storage systems and for memorising techniques for students to use after they have met new language. It would also be quite natural, occasionally, when a new word comes up, to stop briefly during a lesson to think up a good way of remembering it. For example, if we imagine that the word *lavender* has come up and that students find it hard to remember that in English the stress is on the first syllable, you might suddenly think that if you say, 'Lavender! Love it!', this might help pronunciation. You can ask students if they have any ideas of their own for good ways of remembering it too. They will come up with all sorts of imaginative ways of remembering the sound, sight, meaning and use of language – once, that is, they see you think this is a very acceptable way of working and not somehow trivial or cheating!

If you would like to learn some famous techniques for improving memory generally, see O'Brien (2005).

The ways of working exemplified in this chapter hold some implications for lesson planning. These are discussed in more detail in chapter 3.

2.1 Learning a language is like … ?

> Building concepts

Focus: Helping students to have a long-term view of their attempts to learn a new language. Vocabulary depending on the metaphor chosen (see step 1).

Level: Intermediate

Time: 10 minutes

Materials/Preparation: None.

in class

1. Once students have been learning English for some time, at some point in each of several lessons suggest or elicit an analogy or metaphor for learning a new language. You could use *swimming* or *building a house* or *making a garden* or *owning a pet* or anything that you think reflects their age and life experience and that also represents a fairly long-term project which has its ups and downs.

2. Discuss with the students ways in which the chosen analogy is the same or different from language learning, e.g. students might say for *swimming* that it is similar to language learning because you are surrounded by a strange medium, sometimes you feel like you are drowning and it feels like a competition as some people in the class are better at it than others. You don't get wet, though!

3. The ideas connected to the metaphor you choose can be stored on a poster on the wall labelled, e.g., *Learning a language is like swimming.*

4. When things either get tough later on (e.g. when students find something difficult to understand or have trouble memorising something) or when there are delights and successes, you can go back to the poster, ask students what they feel like and what experience they are having, and again relate this to the chosen metaphor.

Follow-up / Variations

A Another time, ask students to offer or to choose a different analogy and work that through carefully, too. Again, write up and store the resulting ideas under a heading. This way you gradually accumulate several posters displaying useful ideas about the experience of learning a language.

2.1 Learning a language is like … ?

B Students can be encouraged to come up with metaphors for other areas of language learning such as *Good questions* or *Clear thinking*.

Note
See also the 'Learning dip and rise', activity 1.6.

2.2 Question matrix

> Building concepts

Focus: Finding out what students would like to know about a topic before you get into it. Helping students to take responsibility for their own questions rather than always expecting the teacher to provide answers. Question formation.

Level: Elementary upwards

Time: 10 minutes at the start of class

Materials/Preparation: None.

in class

1. Write up in the middle of the board the name of the area you want to start working on, and then draw lots of radiating spokes coming out of this central topic. The topic could be:
   - a grammatical area, e.g. *verb tenses for storytelling*,
   - a vocabulary area, e.g. *words for physical ailments*,
   - a functional area, e.g. *broaching a difficult request to a host family*,
   - a writing skill, e.g. *writing a review of a film or CD*,
   - a real world topic such as *body piercing*,
   - a unit of a course book, e.g. *Module 3*, or
   - anything else you plan to work on.

2. Tell students that you would like to know what they don't know or what they want to know about this topic. You might start off with a very easy question yourself first. Say it out loud and then write it up at the end of a spoke, e.g. you could write up, 'What sort of stories will we be doing?' or 'What is an ailment?' or 'Why do we have to learn about review writing?' or 'How many people in this room have got body piercings?' depending on the topic in the centre of the board. Put your initials next to your question.

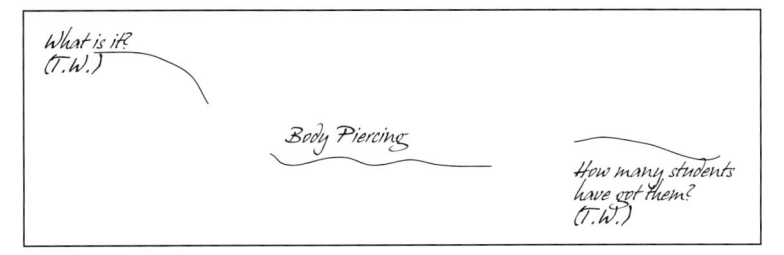

   ```
   What is it?
   (T.W.)
                    Body Piercing
                                    How many students
                                    have got them?
                                    (T.W.)
   ```

3. Wait for a student to call out a question, make sure it is correctly worded, and then write it up with the student's initials by it.

2.2 Question matrix

4. Repeat steps 2 and 3 until you get questions from different students. If you don't get many, you might wonder whether the topic or the way it is expressed on the board is clear or interesting enough for the class. But usually, if your wait-time is good and you accept the early questions gracefully, more questions will come. You can use the waiting time to make a note of the questions raised so far and the initials of the students who asked them.

5. Finally, ask any extra questions you think are really fundamental to the topic and write them up too.

6. Ask the class to write down the question matrix in their notebooks. Also, make sure that any student who has asked a question puts a star by it in their notebook to show that they own it. Make your own copy too of who asked what.

7. Explain that, later on in the term, you will call on different students to say or write whether they think their question has been answered and, if so, what the answer or partial answer seems to be.

Follow-up
1. You now know who is interested in what. When you are about to deal with an area of the main topic that touches on someone's question, you can look back at your notes to refresh your mind as to who it was and say something like, 'Now this will help to answer your question, Petra!'

2. Try to make sure that you do feed in answers to all the questions asked, whether you do this by asking students to do research, or by providing answers in course materials and discussion yourself.

3. Later, ask students to tell the class or to make a poster or write in their dialogue journals what they think they have learned about their own questions. You do not have to grade this work.

Variations
A Students can ask other people, e.g. friends, relatives and other students, what questions they have on a particular topic, and bring those to class

B Instead of taking responsibility for one or two questions, students can choose a whole topic and take responsibility for, say, producing a portfolio on the topic later on in their school career. Again, this work need not be graded and students can stop when they want.

Acknowledgement
My thanks to Kieran Egan for these variations.

2.3 Concept sheets

> Building concepts

Focus: Helping students to understand what they are learning, and to realise that to learn something you may need to meet it several times. To see the progress they have achieved over time.

Level: Elementary upwards

Time: 5-10 minutes at the end of a learning session

Materials/Preparation: One sheet per student per concept and some spares for students who need to start again (see next page for example).

in class

1. Show the students the blank concept sheets and explain that you will be using them to help them to know what they are learning, why they are learning it and how their learning develops over time.

2. After a learning session, help the students to fill in a blank concept sheet each. Make sure they leave plenty of space for later learning.

3. Ask students to store the sheets in a special place in their folders or notebooks.

Follow-up / Variations

A When you next want to work on the concept, one of your options will be to ask students to get out their concept sheets. Once they have reviewed what they learned last time, have met the concept again and have learned a bit more, they can write this additional understanding on the same concept sheet together with the date of the second meeting.

B You may well want to edit the headings in the sheet below. For example, you could add *Useful diagrams* if you use a lot of timelines etc in your classes. You could add sections such as *My favourite mistakes* or *What is it the same as?* or *What is this NOT?* or *How do I know that I know this?*, or anything else you feel would be useful for your students.

2.3 Concept sheets

Example sheet (partially filled in)

Name of what I am learning ___Present Simple tense___

1st meeting (date) ___25th October 2010___

2nd meeting (date) _____

3rd meeting (date) _____

Why am I learning this? ___So I can talk about what I do every day or often or sometimes___

What does it mean? ___A habit or something regular___

What does it look like? ___Questions: do I/you/we/they? does s/he? plus infinitive without 'to' Answers Yes, I do. No, I don't___

___Yes, s/he does. No, s/he doesn't___

What does it sound like? ___Duzzy? Dushy? Dozeye?___

Where is it often found? ___In talk when finding out about people___

What is it often found with? ___Words like sometimes, often, never, always___

What are the rules?

Examples

___I feed my rabbit every day in the morning. My mum feeds her at night.___

2.4 Concept stretching

> Building concepts

Focus: Helping students to be sure that they understand something and also keep on developing their understanding.

Level: Elementary upwards

Time: 5–7 minutes max each lesson

Materials/Preparation: Look back at an activity in which the students have made a concept sheet (for step 1).

in class

1. Ask students about one of the concepts they have been learning and for which they have made a concept sheet (see activity 2.3). You can ask questions about the form or meaning or use of the concept, by asking, e.g.:
    'Can I say *I get up at seven yesterday morning*?'
    'Can I say *I gets up at 8*?'
    'Is it okay for me to ask *Do you earn a lot of money*?'
    'What is the Present Simple all about?'
    'Is it the same as anything else you know?'
    'How is it different from other things we have learned?'
   Ask the questions in a gentle, exploratory way.

2. When you get an answer to the question you have chosen to ask, go on to ask 'Why?' or 'Why not?' Explore what the students say in a genuinely interested way. Show students that it is okay if they get things slightly wrong or have not quite understood. The time spent on this activity gives them a chance to refine the concepts they are learning.

Follow-up / Variations
The following example of a way of working on concept stretching with non-language-based topics comes from James Nottingham's web site www.challenginglearning.com (see also Nottingham, 2010).

A Start by selecting a topic. Write it in the centre of the board. Topics could be *Dreams*, *Friends*, *Home*, *Originality*, *Beauty*, *Rich*, *Real*, *Escape*, or *Lies*. You can always start concept stretching with a *What is...?* question, e.g. 'What is lying?'
When the students respond, challenge them by either questioning their assumptions, testing their conclusions or asking one of the suggested questions below. In the mother tongue, this works even

2.4 Concept stretching

with very young children, from the age of four onwards. For English language learners, try it from Intermediate level upwards. Here is a fuller example.
- Tell an outrageous lie, for example, 'My name is Sam and I'm a hairy gruffalo', but say it with a smile on your face.
- When the students say that's not true, ask the class, for example, 'How can you tell if someone is telling a lie?' Students may say, 'Because they smile when they talk.' You then ask, 'So if I smile whilst I'm talking, am I lying?' and then say something that is very obviously true, but with a smile on your face. Next, you could ask, 'What if I do this? (*frown*) Am I telling the truth?' Then say something that is very obviously false, but with a frown on your face.

Work this way in good humour, but gently challenging the students' assumptions. Here are some further questions you could ask.
- Is it always wrong to tell lies? (Even if it's to avoid hurting someone's feelings?)
- If I pretend to be a rabbit, am I telling lies?
- If you tell your mother that you haven't bought her a present when you have, is that lying?
- Is it lying to say there is a tooth fairy? (for older children only!)

B Share the choice of topic and the question-making with the participants.

C It is always a good idea to encourage transfer by asking students how they think the work they have just been doing on a particular concept, whether *Past Simple* or *Transition* or *Outsiders*, relates to what they are learning in other school subjects or what they are doing outside school.

Note
To prepare for activities 2.6–2.10, choose the topic *Patterns* at stage A.

2.5 Refining vocabulary

> Building concepts

Focus: Refining understanding of recently learned words and phrases.

Level: Pre-Intermediate upwards

Time: 25 minutes

Materials/Preparation: After your class has met some words and phrases and learned them for homework, make a list of them and write them on separate slips of paper; you will need enough to have two slips for every three or four students in your class.

in class

1. Explain that the activity you are going to do next will help students to further their understanding of words and phrases met recently. It is a learning activity.

2. Divide the class into teams of three or four people each. Ask each team to think of a name for their team. Write the names of the teams on the board or on a poster where you can later record their scores.

3. As a dry run, and using an example word or phrase, show the class how, without ever saying the word or phrase, you can help them to guess it. You can, for example, tell students the lesson where they met the word, the word class and the meaning. You can give examples, synonyms and antonyms, use mime and gesture, and make noises to help them guess it. So, if your target word is *elephant* you can say, 'This is a noun. It's an animal. We learned it on Friday. Big ears, grey. Has one of these (wave your arm around like a trunk). Sounds like this (trumpet!).' Whoever puts up their hand and, when asked, says *elephant* would get points for their team once the game has really started.

4. Hand each team a slip of paper with a different word or phrase on it that you want to review and refine. They should keep the slips secret from other teams.

5. Give a time limit for teams to prepare an explanation. Remind them that from now on they must not say the word or phrase on their slips out loud.

2.5 Refining vocabulary

6. When the time is up invite one team to explain their word in any way they like. If you realise that the defining team has got something wrong, e.g. word class or meaning, correct them and be enthusiastic about the new learning that is going on. It is the real reason for the activity.

7. If someone in a different team puts their hand up and guesses the item right, the defining team gets two points for a good explanation and the person who guessed correctly gets one point for their team.

8. Record the scores.

9. Continue the activity until each team has had a chance to explain the word or phrase on their slip of paper.

10. If you have time, you can hand out another round of slips of paper.

11. Once you have briefly celebrated the scores, reinforce the learning points and make sure these are recorded in student vocabulary notebooks.

12. If you wish, you can teach some games language such as *to have a dry run*, *to have a go*, *to beat someone (hollow)*, *to have a return match*.

Variation
Once students have got the hang of the activity and understood its potential for ironing out misunderstandings, they can write on slips of paper the words or phrases they particularly want to review in this way. You can then hand these out to other teams.

2.6 Things of this shape

> Looking for patterns

Focus: Working on seeing similarities between things based on unusual categorising principles. Building up stocks of concrete nouns, adjectives and words for describing shapes.

Level: Elementary upwards

Time: 5–10 minutes.

Materials/Preparation: None.

in class

1. Draw five numbered circles on the board (see below). The smallest circle should be barely visible from where the students are sitting and the largest as big as your board can accommodate. Add two or three more numbers to hint at circles too big to draw on the board and indicate these by gesture.

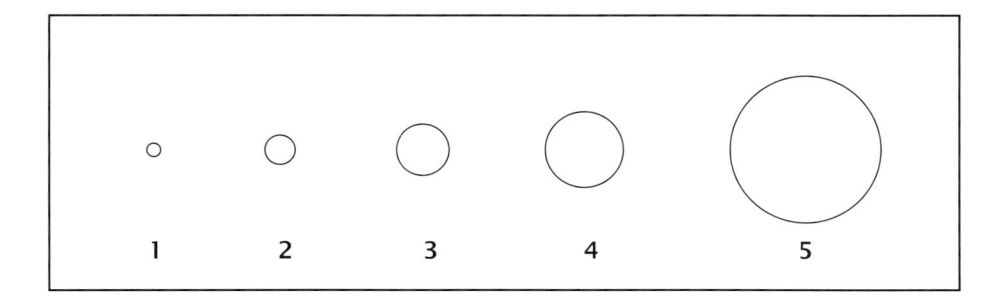

```
   o    ○    ◯    ◯    ◯
   1    2    3    4    5
```

2. On a sheet of paper each student writes the numbers of the circles and by each number the name of any roundish or spherical thing they can think of that is the size of the circle in question. They cannot use words like *big* or *small*. Thus for circle 2 they could write *pea*, but not *little apple*

3. Students can call out ideas or ask you or come to the board to write their words near or in the appropriate circles. Thus for the figure above, you might gradually accumulate words from left to right like *speck of dust, pea, mothball, golf ball, apple, grapefruit, globe of the world, boulder, the moon.*

2.6 Things of this shape

Follow-up / Variations

A On different days, draw different shapes and collect different words, for example squares (postage stamps to cornfields), rectangular planes (cigarette papers to the Canadian province of Manitoba), cubes (sugar cubes to blocks of flats), cylinders (toothpicks to the Channel Tunnel), cones (ice cream cones to Mount Fuji) and so on.

B Once you have done some shapes, branch out into different categories, not worrying necessarily about size any more, e.g. *containers* might give you *suitcase, flower vase, bread bin, glasses case, stable, house*; *frames* might give you *picture frame, door frame, window frame, clothes hanger*.

2.7 Small collections

> Looking for patterns

Focus: Building vocabulary, learning more about each other, looking for similarities and differences.

Level: Any

Time: 5–15 minutes

Materials/Preparation: To start the activity off, three or four specimens of something you have several of at home (see step 1 for ideas).

in class

1. Bring in anything of which you have three or four specimens, for instance, sweaters, earrings, fridge magnets, baskets, fishing lures, spoons.

2. The class suggests ways in which the things are the same, for example, about a sweater: two arms, no buttons, made of wool, a head hole. Help with vocabulary if necessary.

3. The class suggests way in which they are different, for example, blue v green, thick v thin, plain v striped, size 12 v 14.

4. Review in pairs: student A describes – not necessarily in full sentences – one of the objects without looking at it, and B points to the one they think has been described.

Follow-up / Variations

A Students, one by one, over time, bring in objects of which they have three or four, e.g. glasses, mobile phones, striped T shirts. A different student each time takes it in turn to lead the activity.

B Students can write descriptions of unwanted objects within certain categories. They hand the texts in for correction and then these, once corrected, make a class eBay or other auction house catalogue. Students can then organise a class auction.

C Students can also collect things connected to learning English such as their favourite mistakes (see activity 1.7), or instances of objects referred to as masculine or feminine (e.g. 'She (the boat) was loaded to the gunwales').

2.7 Small collections

Notes
Although, theoretically, the interest in collecting things is supposed to peak at about seven years old, I know of many adults of all ages who also get a harmless and pleasant feeling of control over reality by collecting ties, CDs, salt and pepper pots shaped like vegetables etc.

2.8 Clap, listen, clap

> Looking for patterns

Focus: Students listening to each other, trying to recognise sound patterns and thus becoming more sensitive to word and sentence stress.

Level: Elementary upwards

Time: 5–10 minutes

Materials/Preparation: None.

in class

1. Ask students to stand up, listen to you clapping and then clap exactly the same sound pattern themselves.

2. Clap a short sequence with one or two stronger, louder or stressed sounds in it, e.g. ■ ■■■.

3. Wait until students have listened to your sequence and copied it by clapping it themselves correctly. Then repeat steps 2 and 3 a couple of times with different patterns.

4. Next, invite a student to clap a different pattern from yours; ask the others to listen carefully and then repeat the pattern the student clapped.

5. Ask different individual students to clap, and the class to listen and copy. If you have a small class, you can simply go round the room one by one. If you have a bigger class, call out the first student's name and then ask that student to choose the next clapper and so on.

Follow-up / Variations
Once students have got the idea and are getting good at copying accurately, you can choose one of the students' clapping patterns, and once people have copied it you can ask them to shout out any English word they think has the same pattern. So if someone clapped ■ ■■, students could call out, e.g., *vegetable, comfortable, animal, elephant, beautiful* etc.

Acknowledgement
I learned this from Ferdinand Stefan.

2.9 Odd one(s) out

> Looking for patterns

Focus: Helping students to think about and notice the characteristics of pieces of language, and the similarities and differences between language items. The activity can be used to see how much students know before or after a module of work or for assessment. The language of opinions, comparison and contrast and reasoning can also be a strong focus.

Level: Pre-Intermediate upwards

Time: 30–60 minutes

Materials/Preparation: You need to identify the particular concepts and principles of categorisation you wish to work on (e.g. the different sounds of Past Simple verb endings or the differences between formal and informal language). Then prepare a data set for students to analyse where some items share the principle but others do not (see examples in variation D).

in class

1. Elicit or pre-teach the language of opinions, comparison and contrast, and giving reasons, so that later, students will be able to say things like, 'I think these two are the same because …', 'Yeah, but this one is different because …', 'This is more … and … less …'
2. Give students alone, in pairs or in small groups, the same sets of data. The data can be as few as three items and as many as thirty, depending on their length and type. The data items can be words, phrases, sentences, or utterances. These can be gathered from the course book, a concordance sampling, corrected homework, a dictionary, an audio or video tape, newspapers or any other source of the target language.
3. Ask students to consider which items are the same and why, and which ones are different and why.

Follow-up / Variations

A Different groups of students can be given different data sets and items to discuss.

B Students can be asked to state the similarities between items in the main set as well as the differences between it and the odd one(s) out.

C Students can find data and write their own lists for others to

2.9 Odd one(s) out

discuss. You can support this work by giving them some examples to start them off and by asking for a small set of items. Students can then collect their items, underline the odd one(s) out, write down their reasons and hand this in for correction.

D Data sets can be about one particular feature of grammar, phonology, register, meaning, spelling, etc. Here are some examples.
  1. Pronunciation
     Data sets such as: *snake, last, silly, shell* or *church, ancient, German, choose* can be used to firm up pronunciation of difficult sounds.
  2. Word class
     A data set such as: *chilly, raining, cold, cool, wind, warm, boiling* can provide more than one odd one out and more than one reason.
  3. Singular/plural
     A data set such as: *children, horse, geese, apples, accommodation, roof, fish* could be used.

E Once students have become familiar with this sort of exercise the data sets can contain phrases or sentences, can be bigger and can be about more than one feature.
Even a data set as short as the following one on register: *Hi, Hiya, Morning, All right?, Good morning, See you, How do you do?, Ta ta, Cheers,* can provide several different classifications of utterance and many different reasons for them, e.g. time of day, first or second meeting, formal or neutral or informal register, international or regional distribution, topic (simple greeting or asking about health).

F You can make a large data set composed of 30 items or more and use it on different occasions to sensitise students to different features.

G You can use the idea of the Odd One Out with texts that contain nonsensical, illogical or incongruent items. So, for example, students would have to spot the odd things about a text such as, 'One morning Sally went to school at about 4 pm. It was really cold, so she wore a sleeveless T shirt.' For contradictory stories like this see Frank et al (1982) p. 33.

H All the odd one out ideas above can be used with data sets that are NOT specifically about language, for example, about trees and flowers, food and drink, animals and people, types of government or dramatic arts or different sorts of philosophical argument. Used with these topics, the idea is useful for building vocabulary about concrete or abstract things and their attributes.

2.9 Odd one(s) out

Acknowledgement
Although this is a very familiar EFL activity often done at word level with vocabulary sets (e.g. *pear, apple, potato, banana, peach*) Lin and Mackay (2004, pp. 21-31) have developed Odd One Out into a really useful tool for thinking.

2.10 Like WHAT??!!

> Looking for patterns

Focus: This activity encourages students to analyse topics, see similarities and differences between apparently unconnected topics, represent these graphically and then recombine elements creatively in order to come up with interesting ideas. It involves vocabulary related to the topics you choose (see below), and practice of the Present Simple tense. Step 7 encourages use of the second conditional.

Level: Intermediate upwards

Time: 30–60 minutes

Materials/Preparation: You need two topics which seem very different from each other (see step 1), slips of paper and some A3 paper for step 5.

in class

1. Put students in pairs. Give pairs in one half of the class a slip of paper each, on which is written the same topic, e.g. *a student*. Give pairs in the other half of the class a slip of paper each, on which is written a different topic, e.g. *a wild animal*. Do not explain that there are thus two topics in the room. Students will probably assume that everyone has the same topic. If they do, it gives a nice element of surprise to step 3.

2. Ask students, in pairs, to think of all the things the topic does, eats and wears, what it looks like, what it does at the weekend etc. In other words, how you would recognise or know the topic. Give an example that makes sense for both topics, e.g. *eats meat, sleeps a lot, walks around in the daytime*. Explain that both people in the pair need to write down the ideas they generate.

3. Once students have written down about seven things, stop them. Re-pair students so that each person now sits down with someone who has the other topic. So a *student* topic person sits with a *wild animal* topic person.

4. Ask them now to help each other to extend their separate lists. Ask them to see if by helping each other they can get to ten items for both topics.

5. Next, give each student a large piece of paper and ask them to draw a big Venn diagram, i.e. two intersecting circles.

2.10 Like WHAT??!!

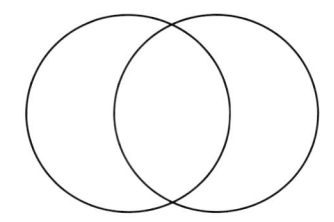

One big circle is labelled *Student* and the other *Wild Animal*. Show this on the board. In the central overlapping section they should help each other to write things that the two topics have in common, e.g. *sleeps a lot* or *walks around by day*. In the separate sections, they write ideas that fit into the specific topics, e.g. *eats people* in the Wild Animal circle section and *watches TV* in the Student circle section. As they do this they can add new ideas that they have not thought of before.

6. Once students have had time to do this, pull lots of example ideas from them and record some onto the board. You can ask, 'What does a student do (or wear / like / dislike etc) that a wild animal does not?' or 'What do both these creatures do / like / dislike?' As the ideas come up, offer if necessary more precise vocabulary or refine the language. Students expand and correct their own work on their own sheets of paper as you go.

7. You now have a corrected version of a large, filled-in Venn diagram on the board, and students have their own copy too. Next, ask students to think of how a wild animal could be more like a student or a student more like a wild animal! Give them a minute to think, and then accept their answers in the same spirit as you accepted their 'Thunk' answers (see activity 1.11). You may get ideas such as 'A wild animal in a zoo feels like me in school!' or 'If students ate their teachers, they would be more like a wild animal!' Enjoy the ideas that come up, and then ask students, either in class or for homework, to write down three to seven more ways in which these two topics could be more like each other.

Follow-up
Take in the homework. Correct it and read out the funniest, most perceptive, most unusual ideas to the class next lesson. Alternatively, good ideas can be stored on a classroom poster and kept on the wall as an example of creative thinking.

Variations
You can use this idea with very different topics on different days, e.g. *Teacher/Artist, Lesson/Meal, Exam/Science Experiment*.

Notes
Listing items in different categories and then combining and recombining items from lists in different categories is a classic creativity tool. (See chapter 5 for more on creative thinking.)

2.11 Physical storage

> Memorising

Focus: Helping students to keep track of new language in an organised and helpful way.

Level: Any

Time: 10 minutes each lesson

Materials/Preparation: Depends on the storage method used (see next page).

in class

1. Encourage students to work with any of the following storage systems by initially showing them an example, and then providing materials and guidance so that they can start to make and use them on their own.

2. Then allow time for the system(s) to be used in class and also set homework tasks that involve their use.

Follow-up / Variations
Students can later be asked to regroup the same items in different ways, e.g. to re-order them by alphabetical order, word class, usefulness in different spheres of life or other criteria that you and they dream up.

Note
The acts of making, adding to and then using these storage items will help students to meet and re-meet target items often and to consider salient features such as their form, meaning, use and personal significance.

2.11 Physical storage

Systems can include:

Lists
For short items, students can write lists of target items and their translations or lists of *words I like* and *words I don't like* or *words with the same number of syllables*. Extra information about word class, association and main stress can be coded onto the lists.

Cards
A useful old idea is for students to write down target items on one side of a piece of card and to record other information such as meaning or translation, on the other side.

Mind maps
These can be made on topics areas of useful vocabulary (e.g. *my house*). They can show the difference between main topics (such as different rooms: *bedroom, bathroom, lounge*) and minor areas of the rooms (*near window, on bed, near bed, storage places* etc). Vocabulary can then be stored in the appropriate place (thus near the phrase *on bed* we could write the words, e.g. *mattress, pillow, sheets, duvet*).

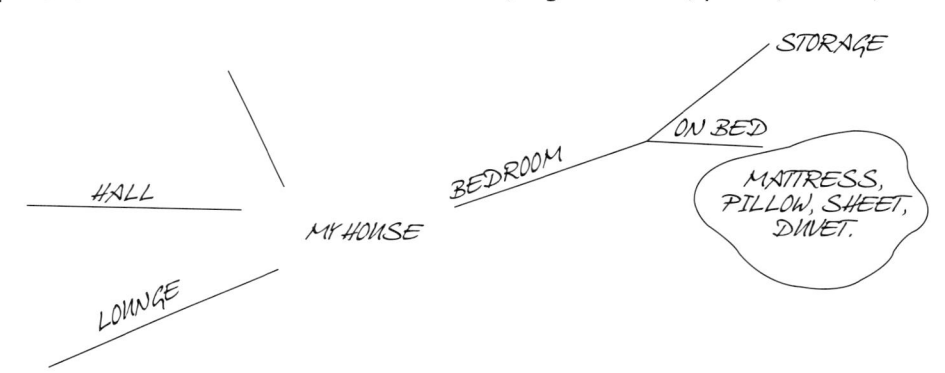

[Mind map diagram: MY HOUSE branching to HALL, LOUNGE, BEDROOM; BEDROOM branching to STORAGE and ON BED; ON BED containing MATTRESS, PILLOW, SHEET, DUVET.]

Scales
Bi-polar scales can be used to plot out grades of meaning difference. Spaces can be left for later learning. For example, to store adverbs of frequency a scale could look like this:

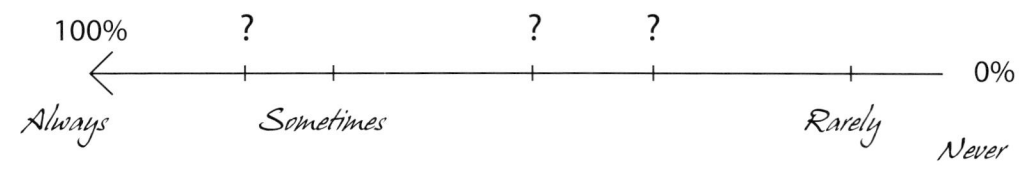

[Scale diagram from 100% to 0%: Always, ?, Sometimes, ?, ?, Rarely, Never]

Posters
Posters of different sizes, shapes and colours can be used to group together language of, e.g., similar topic, sound, sight, meaning, use. The posters can be displayed on the classroom wall, in a student's bedroom at home or on the back of a door.

2.12 Mnemonics

> Memorising

Focus: Helping students to come up with imaginative memory pegs to hang new language on.

Level: Elementary upwards

Time: 1–3 minutes at different moments

Materials/Preparation: None.

in class

1. Encourage students to experiment with any of the mnemonic devices or strategies below.

2. Show how useful these are by telling students how you use them yourself. So, for example, when teaching the first letter or acronym method, you can tell them that you remember the colours of the rainbow by saying 'ROY G BIV' to yourself to help you remember red, orange, yellow … green … blue, indigo, violet.

3. Encourage students to tell you their own personal mnemonic devices and examples too.

2.12 Mnemonics

Here are some useful mnemonic devices:

Link words
The link words technique involves using words in both the target language and mother tongue to construct an unusual mental picture. Williams and Burden (1997, p. 17) give the example of the French word *nappe*, meaning tablecloth, which can be remembered by an English speaker if they make a mental picture of someone having a nap on a tablecloth.

Mental images
Students can create unusual mental images of a target language item, e.g. they can imagine it pink, or huge, or shrink it or make it seem very far away.

Sound and movement images
If the target item is onomatopoeic, i.e. it sounds like it means, students can say it out loud in that manner, e.g. 'POP!' or 'SPLASH!'
If the item is movement connected, do the movement at the same time as saying the word, e.g. mime pushing a door really hard while saying 'Push! Push hard! Push again! Push harder!'

Step it out
Using fingers on desks or standing up and using real walking steps, students can 'step out' the rhythm of a word or phrase, e.g. *typical!* will involve one long stride and two short ones.

Tracing
Students can trace a word that they find difficult to spell up in the air with their fingers. Neuro-linguistic programming experts would say that if they do this above their heads and to the left, they will remember it better. If you work in a Steiner school and have in your room a sand tray or some different textured materials such as velvet, sandpaper, silk, wax and velcro, students can trace the letters out on the texture they think fits the word best, e.g. a student might choose to trace out *furious* on sandpaper because it feels rough and nasty, and that is how you feel when you are furious.

Meaning images
Students can make little spelling pictures that show the meaning of the word, e.g.:

```
        T     U
     N    A  O  S
   U        I N
  O
  M
```

2.13 Rehearsal

> Memorising

Focus: Finding interesting ways for students to meet the target items over and over again and to gain skill and speed in recalling how to say them, read them and use them well for their own purposes.

Level: Any

Time: 5–10 minutes

Materials/Preparation: None.

in class

1. Once students have started to work on the storage of new language and on creating mnemonic devices, you can present as many of the following ideas to them as appropriate to their level and the time available.

Mnemonic devices
- Repeating language over and over in their heads silently or using it for meaningful purposes, such as conversations, using their 'inner voices', before self-testing (see below).
- Repeating language over and over out loud in different ways, e.g. whispering, speaking slowly, fast, or with different emotions such as sadly or frantically or joyfully.
- Reciting short pieces out loud after learning them off by heart.
- Copying in differing writing styles, e.g. capitals, pencil, keyboard or within different diagrams and shapes, or on pictures.
- Self-testing, e.g. reading or listening to language then seeing if they can say it or write it themselves without looking at or listening to the prompts. If successfully remembered, any small storage item such as a card (see activity 2.11) can go in one pile or pocket and the less well-remembered items can go in another pile or pocket.
- Matching items, e.g. formal phrase with its informal equivalent, word with its meaning, item to mnemonic.
- Finding opposites, e.g. antonyms, target words and meanings of their antonyms.
- Recognising language within a text, word search puzzle, or dialogue and, at the moment of recognition, underlining it, putting a hand up or standing up.

2.14 Mime round the circle

> Memorising

Focus: A playful way of increasing student-to-student attention and concentration, and improving memory. Gentle physical relaxation. Noticing and accommodating classmates, which is the start of teambuilding. Vocabulary building.

Level: Elementary upwards

Time: 10 minutes

Materials/Preparation: None.

in class

1. Ask students to stand by their desks. If you have a small class of, say, 15 or so, and enough room, students can stand in a circle.

2. Explain that, in a minute, each student will imagine an object but not say it out loud. They will need to show by gesture, mime and expression what the object is, e.g. if they choose an umbrella, they can pretend to look up and see rain falling, show the length of the umbrella and mime opening it up and holding it above their heads. Once they have tried to show the object, they mime passing it to their neighbour. The neighbour then mimes putting it down and starts to mime their own different object. So each student will show a different object and at the end students, in pairs, will try to name in English all the objects they have 'seen'.

3. Give examples of types of things students can show, e.g. sports equipment (bikes, tennis rackets), musical instruments (guitar, violin), things you wear (glasses, earrings), things you carry (lipstick, comb, iPod) etc. Let students come up with other examples and show them how precise their gestures and mimes need to be in order to be clear to others.

4. Start off with a clear mime of, say, a bouncing ball and then 'pass it' to the next person.

5. Once students have all had a go at miming an object and passing it on, let them try to remember in pairs all the things they have seen. Elicit the object vocabulary (e.g. *umbrella*, *ball*, *mirror*) and at higher levels the verb too (e.g. *to open an umbrella*, *to bounce a ball*, *to look in a mirror*).

2.15 Eight-step memorising procedure

> Memorising

Focus: This eight-step procedure can be used to help students memorise almost any poem, text, dialogue, story or other stretch of target language.

Level: Pre-Intermediate upwards

Time: 30 minutes, depending on the length of the target stretch of language

Materials/Preparation: See below.

in class

1. **Slow reveal**
   Choose a stimulus such as a text, a set of pictures for a story, a poem, a recipe or other appropriate material for your class. Do not give the whole stimulus out immediately; students need to work hard at getting it so that they become curious, and get involved. This will make it more memorable. Students can work at revealing a stimulus in any of the following ways:
   - guessing contents from a given title
   - selecting and then sorting jumbled pictures, words, sentences, or ideas into a possible order and adding their own suggestions
   - asking Yes/No questions to the teacher from key word prompts given on the board
   - filling in gaps using hints given by the teacher
   - guessing what is in the part of a picture that is partially masked.

   Once students have got very close to guessing the stimulus, reveal most of it. Allow time for students to compare their predictions with reality.

2. **Comprehension**
   Once the stimulus is available to students (though see step 7), make sure in your usual ways that they understand it fully before getting into the language aspects.

3. **Noticing**
   See activity 2.11 for ways in which salient features of target language can be made noticeable.
   Here is an extra way of helping students to notice things about a text. Read it out loud to them while they follow the text by reading silently. But change the occasional word or phrase. So if

the text says *The woman took a coffee*, you might read out loud, 'The lass helped herself to a coffee'. When students hear that you have changed something, they should underline the part you have changed. Once you have finished reading a section out loud with changes, they work in pairs to agree on which parts you changed and how you changed them. You can then discuss with students what difference, if any, is created by each change in wording.

4. **Rehearsal**
Students next try to commit the target stretch of language to memory. Using picture, word, sound or gesture prompts to help them, they can do this by saying short stretches out loud, building forwards into longer stretches, and doubling back to review past stretches thus recycling constantly. They can work with a partner to say alternate lines out loud then switch roles to commit the other lines to memory. Half the class can say one half of the text and the other half the other.

5. **Removal**
While the students are rehearsing as in step 4, any picture or word prompts can gradually be removed.

6. **Reproduction**
Next, give students time to write the target stretch of language down and to check that they have it correct.

7. **Surprise**
Tell students that in fact there is still a little piece of the stimulus remaining. Ask them to predict what the rest of it is like. Reveal the final part of the stimulus and see whose prediction was closest. Then work with the final part of the stimulus as before in steps 2–6, and continue with step 8 below.

8. **Crazy questions**
Ask unusual questions such as 'How many lines are there?' 'How many times does the letter *K* or the word *state* appear?' 'How many words are there in the first line/sentence?' 'How much would the contents cost?' 'What would a hairdresser/TV news person/single mother/ remember/think/say about it?' Or ask students to say the piece out loud line by line, but backwards!

Follow-up / Variations
Another day, ask students to work together to remember the target stretch of language without looking at their notebooks. Don't treat it like a test, but give them lots of help by prompting when they get stuck, e.g. 'Remember how many lines there were in the first section?' 'Remember how many times the word *state* appeared?' 'What was the word that rhymed with *night*?'

2.15 Eight-step memorising procedure

Note
This activity brings together a lot of the ideas mentioned earlier, such as using a meaningful story context, semantic grouping, visual aids, physical storage, rehearsal, student collaboration. Memorisation is the foundation of speed of recall and processing and thus of the automaticity fundamental to fluent speech.

2.16 Guided picture composition

> Memorising

Focus: This is an example of an eight-step memorising procedure (see previous activity).

Level: Pre-Intermediate upwards

Time: 20–40 minutes, depending on length of composition you want students to write

Materials/Preparation: A guided picture composition. For this, you need a set of pictures or a cartoon strip that tells a story that you think will amuse or interest your learners. Make as many photocopies of the set as you have students. Cut off the punch line pictures, and jumble the rest, keeping them in sets, one for each student.

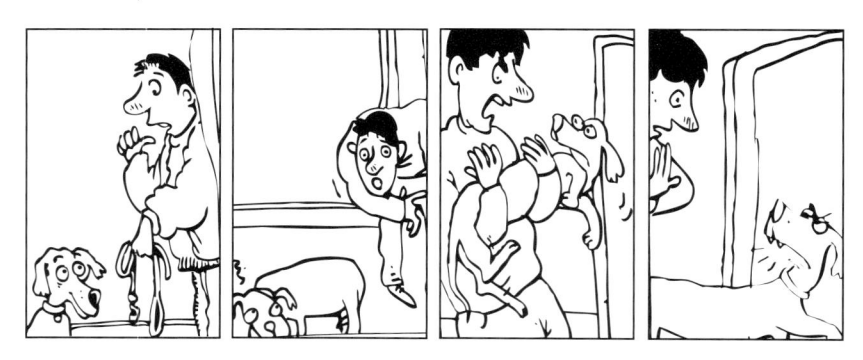

in class

1. **Slow reveal** Give a set each of the jumbled pictures to individuals, pairs or small groups of students. Ask them to look through the pictures and put them in a possible order. Discuss the possible orders with the class, asking them to justify their sequences. Once you have all agreed a good order, ask students to number the pictures.

2. **Comprehension** Write the numbers of the pictures up on the board with space underneath them. Start work on the first picture. Elicit from students ideas about, e.g., the name and setting of the main character. Write up prompts on the board under the number 1 to help students to remember these ideas. Thus, if your picture story is about a man taking a dog for a walk, you might elicit the ideas *next door neighbour*, *Fred*, *dog*, *Spot*. Put these words up together with any little helpful phrases that students come up with, such as *every morning* or *to take the dog for a walk*.

2.16 Guided picture composition

3. **Noticing** If students come up with rather easy language or with incorrect language, you can extend it or correct it and then star or underline on the board anything you particularly want them to notice. So, for example, if you want the story to be in Past Simple, write this and the words *Last Saturday morning* clearly on the board, and point to it any time a student makes an avoidable mistake with the tense of their offering. If you want students to use a variety of time linkers (such as *and then, later on, a bit later, after ...ing*), you could write a list down one side of the board so that they can choose from the range as they go through the story. If you want students to get used to thinking in terms of lexical variation, you could list words to use instead of *the dog*, e.g. *the mongrel, the animal, the creature, his pet, Spot*. Again, as they go through the story, students can choose from this list.

4. **Rehearsal** Once you have some notes up on the board about the first picture, ask a student to tell that part of the story from memory using the board prompts. It's not a test, so ask others to help if the student falters. Once it is correct, you can ask another student or the whole class to repeat it.
Work on picture 2 in the same way. Once students have got a good sentence or two for picture 2, ask them to loop back and tell the story from picture 1, the beginning, again.
Keep working in the same way, i.e., help students to tell the part of the story connected to the next new picture, and once they can do this, ask them to loop back to the beginning or to an earlier picture to tell more of the earlier part of the story. To vary the procedure here you can ask individuals, pairs, groups or half the class to loop back and tell the story from the start.

5. **Removal** While the students are rehearsing as above you can gradually offer less and less help so they are doing more story-telling on their own. If you feel the class is *very* competent, you could remove (some of) the word prompts from the board.

6. **Surprise** (*In this example of the activity, I have switched the order of stages 6 and 7.*) Once students have dealt with all the pictures and can tell the story so far pretty well, let them into the secret that in fact the story doesn't end at the last picture they have; there are in fact more pictures. Ask them to predict what might happen next in the story. You could ask them to do this in pairs and then, after a minute or two, list their ideas on the board. Then hand out the final picture(s) and discuss whose prediction was closest. Work on the final part of the story and the punch line as you did with the earlier pictures.

2.16 Guided picture composition

7. **Reproduction** Next, give students time to write the story down using the pictures and the word prompts, if you have left them on the board. They could finish this off for homework if you wish.

8. **Crazy questions** Finally, ask questions such as 'How many lines are there in your story?' 'How many times does the past of an irregular verb appear?' 'How many different words have you used for *dog*?' Or point to where one of the picture numbers and notes used to be on the board and ask them to use their 'magic eyes' to see what used to be written there. Many students have a somewhat photographic memory and will be able to 'see' what was there.

CHAPTER 3
KEEPING IT PRACTICAL: WAYS OF STRUCTURING LESSONS FOR THINKING

As busy working language teachers, we need to know what the practical implications are of any new ideas or work we have come across.

This chapter thus initially focuses on what implications the ideas in the introduction and first two chapters of this book hold for our lesson planning. It then looks at an unusual type of teacher reflection and at the approach of the English National Curriculum (ENC) and at its implications for lesson structure in any cultural setting. We also consider the use of exploratory talk, a kind of conversation we can use no matter what our lesson plan or structure might be. Finally, the work of the Imaginative Education Research Group (IERG) is explored.

In the introduction to the book, I mentioned that very diverse topics pop up in EFL classes. Topics such as holidays and airports, and restaurants and festivals appear in texts and audio materials, in activities, tasks, songs and poems in course books and in our own materials too. So if we decided to work on the topic of Thinking by including, say, a reading on memorisation techniques or a whole class preparation stage before a formal debate, there would be no need to change our lesson plan or our lesson structure in any way. We could just deal with this topic in the same way we deal with any other, i.e. making sure it is relevant and interesting to our students, and making sure they understand it and that related language is pre-taught or noticed, practised and used.

Teaching Tips

If we decide to work on our *own* behaviour and routines in order to provide a class climate conducive to thinking, as detailed in chapter 1, we might want to change our lesson structure just a little. We might, for example, allow time at the start of the lesson for an advance organiser or a concentration warm-up or a calming exercise. Or we might want to allow time at the end of the lesson for student reflection time. Much of our lesson plan and structure, however, could stay the same as ever.

TT1 Thinking that is fundamental to language learning

If we heed the ideas in chapter 2, we will wish to check that we:
- understand the concepts we are about to teach,
- mediate learning carefully, and
- help students to make sure that they really understand the material introduced, become more alert to patterns generally and notice the patterns in the English language particularly.

We will work with our students on how to memorise material in different ways, too. This implies perhaps some extra teacher preparation beforehand, and some additional steps within the lesson, including perhaps more time allowed for memory work if we don't allow for this already. Generally, however, we will not have to alter our normal lesson structure or plan a great deal.

TT2 Unusual teacher reflection

We could plan and run our lessons in exactly the same way as we usually do, not making any change to the plan or structure whatsoever. But then, after the lesson, the week or the term was over, we could look back at our and our students' work, the lesson tasks and materials, the class discussions and so on, and reflect on them in a slightly different way from normal. Whilst referring to one of the major taxonomies of thinking, (e.g. Bloom's taxonomy, see pp 12–13), we could consider what types of thinking we just happen to have worked on while we have been busy with our normal programme. So again, this would not mean any change at all in our lesson planning or structure. It would mean instead that extra time was needed, after a module or term of teaching, for teacher reflection. It would be, for most of us, a novel way of looking back at our term's work, like putting on a new pair of glasses to look at a familiar scene.

TT3 The English National Curriculum approach

There has been a deliberate attempt to infuse the teaching of thinking into the process of learning a foreign language, a way that involves a complete change of lesson structure. In the National Curriculum of England, five thinking skills, (information processing, reasoning, enquiry, creative thinking and evaluation), are now to be taught to learners in every school subject 'to enable them to learn *how* to learn as well as to know *what* they are learning' (Lin and Mackay 2004). Work has been done to figure out how these five thinking skills can be integrated into modern foreign language teaching and learning in secondary schools in England.[1]

Leat (2008) suggests that a lesson that concentrates on one of the five thinking skills above can have four distinct phases:

i) **The Launch** This is where you establish the reason, importance or relevance of what you are going to do in the lesson. The 'what' you are going to teach will be some kind of thinking. An example might be Evaluating. The launch can involve stories, anecdotes, indeed anything to get students interested. You could, for example, explain that you bought a new pair of running shoes at the weekend and it took ages because you could not make up your mind. You could go on to ask, 'Actually how *do* you make up your mind when you are buying shoes?' This phase can involve linguistic preparation for the intended task below.

ii) **The Instructions** This is where you explain how the task is to be done and set expectations about thinking and learning behaviour, e.g. that students should listen to each other and not be satisfied with the first idea they come up with. A task on Evaluating could involve groups of students having to make a decision about the purchase of something for their school class with a limited budget for a choice of items and, through this work, coming up with some principles for evaluating whether money is well-spent or ill-spent.

iii) **The Hard Thinking** This is where groups collaborate, using 'exploratory talk' (see below), on an open and challenging task or on a problem that has no one, simple, right answer. The teacher will be looking, listening and mediating here. Slower students may need some help with strategies. Speedy students may need to be asked to evaluate their answers, support them with evidence or come up with more alternatives ready for the next stage.

---

1 I am indebted to Dr David Leat, Reader in Curriculum Innovation and Director of the Centre for Learning and Teaching at Newcastle University, for explaining the work being done.

Teaching Tips

iv) **The Debriefing** This is where the teacher and the group explore, by discussion, what they have done and learned, and how they have done it and learned it. The teacher also tries to make connections to other contexts to increase the chances of generalisation and transfer (e.g. the teacher could encourage discussion of when and how students evaluate as a natural everyday process).[2]

As you read through the very different lesson structure above, several things may have occurred to you, as they did to me.

The first and last stages imply, as Leat says, the 'ability to sustain a dialogue with pupils in whole class episodes. In simple terms, this means being able to ask a genuinely open question and respond flexibly and with real interest to what students say in return'. You also need to be able to think on your feet and have good questioning skills.

We discussed questioning skills in the Teaching Tips section of chapter 1. The third stage of the lesson structure above, 'the hard thinking', implies that we teachers thoroughly understand what exploratory talk is (see TT4) and know how to encourage it in students (see activities 3.1–3.3).

The lesson structure above has been devised for use with UK secondary school pupils who mostly share a mother tongue and who are learning a foreign language such as French or Spanish. As we saw above, the types of work in this four-stage lesson imply a *lot* of discussion at all stages. Which language will this discussion take place in? If our priority is the learning of thinking strategies, then students lapsing into mother tongue will not seem such a problem. If our students are advanced, then the discussions will be doable in the target language.

If, however, our students are elementary or intermediate in English and our priority is not so much the teaching of thinking strategies but rather the upping of the percentage of target language used in class, then this four-stage plan may need adapting. Alternatively, we can concentrate on the idea of exploratory talk and consider how we can use that within our own normal lesson structures and lesson plans.

TT4 **Exploratory talk: the use of language for thinking together**

It is important to understand more about 'exploratory talk'. It will

---

[2] For more on the use of this four lesson-stages approach to teaching thinking in modern foreign language classes, see Lin and Mackay (2004).

come in handy when we work with colleagues and with advanced students, but we can also use it, in some cases, even at lower levels.

What is it that makes one conversation a joint, co-ordinated intellectual activity, another a prolonged wrangle and another a cosy chat where everyone feels fine but nobody learns much? Neil Mercer (2000) has done a lot of research on this. He actually uses the term 'interthinking' for the joint, co-ordinated, intellectual activity in which people collectively make sense of experience and solve problems. He suggests that we use exploratory talk in classrooms to do interthinking and that the basics of this kind of talk are that:
- relevant past experience is shared
- there is an invitation to participate in a clear task or goal, and
- people work with each other's ideas to transform them into new understanding.

So in this chapter there are some activities we can use to help ourselves and students to get better at exploratory talk, and to do it in English.

Preparing ourselves to facilitate exploratory talk
If we want to work with exploratory talk, as in activities 3.1, 3.2 and 3.3, it will mean that we don't just instruct or facilitate in our classes but also that we become the potential creators of a community of enquiry. We have flirted with this idea a little in earlier activities (see, e.g., 'Thunks' activity 1.11 and activity 2.2) and especially in chapter 2, in the section on building concepts (see 2.3 and 2.4). Mercer (2000) helps us to take this work further by suggesting that as well as recapping relevant past activities, eliciting relevant knowledge from students and elaborating on replies received from students, we can also use question and answer not just to test students but also to uncover initial levels of student understanding and then adjust our teaching accordingly.

How will we know that exploratory talk has taken place? According to Mercer's research (2000: 154), there will be more occurrences of the words *because, if, why* and *I think* when students engage in exploratory talk. More students will talk, students will listen to each other more, utterances may be longer, and people will explain and give reasons more often. Fisher (2008) has a checklist of dialogic skills (in his Appendix 3), thoughts on how to assess progress in dialogue (in his Appendix 4) and questions to help students to evaluate a discussion (in his Appendix 5).

Gerry Stahl also believes in the distinct contribution of small groups for knowledge learning, using and building. He is working towards a science of cognition by looking at the discourse of collaborative small groups engaged in computer networking in maths teams. His articles (see, for example, Stahl 2010) are freely available at www.gerrystahl.net.

TT5 **Imaginative Education**

This section offers a glimpse into the work of the Imaginative Education Research Group (IERG) on how to recapture energy and vitality in our classes, and it was written in conjunction with Kieran Egan.

As teachers, we tend to receive and accept the knowledge that we want our students to learn as ready-portioned and labelled and packaged up. We might have forgotten where, when and who it came from in the first place. We see it in our students' syllabus, in their text books and exams. We come to think of the textbook as the natural habitat of knowledge, rather than recognise that it is really a product of the hopes, fears and passions of individual people. We tend to deal with its contents in a certain order and very thoroughly until, it could perhaps be said, we squeeze the life out of it.

This is unfortunate, because when there is not a lot of interesting content to think about it is hard for teachers and students to think at all. So, perhaps we need to consider if the content in our lessons is really as interesting, funny, or creative as it could be. If not, can we make it so? How can we make the knowledge we want to work on become engaging to the senses and to the imaginations of all our students, especially young people? For them, much of the content of lessons may seem rather alien, dull and meaningless.

The IERG, led by Kieran Egan, aims to help teachers with this by encouraging us to employ 'cognitive tools' in our work. These tools are ways that young students have available to them to help them learn at different ages. For example, a delight in stories, metaphors, jokes and drama are all cognitive tools that help a child to develop a feel for oral language and for indirect experience. A connection with heroes or an interest in the extremes and limits of experience – as in the Guinness Book of Records – are cognitive tools that aid the development of understanding once students develop literacy. By using the cognitive tools available to our students' minds at different stages of their education, we can make even the driest of subjects vivid and meaningful. (For more on the different kinds of understanding children have at different stages and the cognitive tools associated with each of them, see www.ierg.net.)

Working with Imaginative Education is just as interesting for adults as for children. We already use stories and metaphors in our work, appropriately adjusted for our students' ages and backgrounds (see activities 2.1 and 2.10), for we know this catches the imagination, wakes us all up and contributes to thinking.

So now I'd like to go to an example of a cognitive tool that we do not usually work with, one taken from the IERG web site. It is called 'Association with the Heroic'.

Association with the Heroic is the cognitive tool that enables us to overcome some of the threats involved in facing reality. Remember what it was like when you were ten or eleven years old? You were at the mercy of bus schedules, teachers' requirements and school regulations, parents' commands, dress codes and so on and so on. In fact, just at the time your own ego and sense of independence were beginning to develop, you seemed hemmed in by the endless laws, rules and regulations of others. As adults, especially if we are in a work situation of poor quality, we may still feel much the same way on occasions! By associating with those things or people that have heroic qualities and who have tackled such beasts and won, we gain confidence that we too can face and deal with the real world. We gain heart by taking on those qualities with which we associate. In activities 3.4 and 3.5 there are some practical activities for helping students to associate with the heroic.

TT6 Making the learning of English heroic

The natural power in our minds to form associations is so versatile that the range of objects we can feel for seems limitless: the tenacity of a weed on a stormy rock face, the beauty and power of an animal, the elegance of a mathematical proof – all these can be seen as heroic. As teachers, then, as well as working with the activities above, we can also focus on *any* topic in the curriculum, *and project into it some heroic qualities.*

Let's say that we want students to read more, to engage more deeply with books. We can ask students to read a short story or a graded reader on a subject or theme that really interests them. If our students are completely uninterested in books, however, we may need to go further and help them see what is heroic about books. One might highlight the centuries of work that have created this compact object. Crammed with tiny symbols, it serves as a memory outside of us. It is able to hold a huge amount of information and to bring to us the emotions and experiences of other people in distant times and places. Stretched out, the text of a book might cover twenty miles as a single long line of pages. Tiny punctuation marks and spaces make the crammed pages easy on the eye and have helped to democratise reading. Books have probably had more influence on human affairs than all the wars and kings and queens of history. Well, you can see how we can romanticise an object. We need to highlight it, mark it off

Teaching Tips

from its surroundings, make it something with which students can form an association.

Even a point of English grammar such as the pronoun can be made interesting. Pronouns, such as *she, he, it, we, this* and *ours*, can be thought of as a little bit magical because, for example, they can stand in for someone or something that is not there. They can make us see what they want us to see, whether pulling something close (*this*), holding it at a distance (*that*), making us feel included (*we/us*) or excluding others and making them into enemies (*they/them*).

The useful insight of the IERG, then, is that we can harness the power of naturally occurring ways of thinking and plan our lessons around these. In the current example, we separate out the topic of choice and project into it some heroic qualities. If we are interested in planning a lesson around the idea of associating with the heroic, we might think about questions such as the following:

> *What heroic human qualities are central to the topic I wish to introduce? What emotional images do they evoke? What within the topic can best evoke wonder?*
>
> In order to help students connect emotionally to the material, we need to first identify our own emotional attachment to it. What heroic human quality or emotion – courage, compassion, tenacity, fear, hope, loathing, delight etc – can we identify in the topic? These human qualities help us and our students see the world in human terms and give human meaning to events and ideas in all disciplines. We 'humanise' each topic not to falsify it but to infuse the world with human meaning. This first task is the most difficult part of planning the lesson or unit, since we are asked to *feel* about the topic as well as to think about it:
>
> *How can I shape the lesson or unit?*
> Teaching shares some features with news reporting. Just as the reporter's aim is to select and shape events to bring out clearly their meaning and emotional importance for readers or listeners, so our aim as teachers is to present our topic in a way that engages the emotions and imaginations of our students. So, what will our headline and opening sentence be? How will we reveal the background information?
>
> *What's 'the story' on the topic?*
> If we imagine that we *are* news reporters, we will think about events and information in terms of human interest and engagement. Remember, everything is potentially wonderful! In order to be a good reporter, one needs to think this way about whatever it is one has been sent to report on; that is, the reporter writes about or talks about an incident in a way that somehow

engages the reader's / listener's imagination and emotions. And so, too, the teacher.

What aspects of the topic expose extremes of experience or limits of reality? What is most exotic, bizarre or strange about the topic?
Our students' imaginations are often engaged by the extremes of experience and limits of reality. Their imaginations are drawn to what are the most extreme, bizarre, and generally wacky, features of human experience. They revel in the stuff of the *Guinness Book of World Records*. So we need to identify features of the topic that are extreme, that express limits of human experience. This is the stuff of the superlative – the longest, fastest, shortest, hairiest, most, least (and so on) aspects of the topic.

What ideals and/or challenges to conventions are evident in the content? Through what human emotions can students access the topic?
Think of how a good movie or novel makes aspects of the world engaging. Obstacles to the hero/heroine are humanised in one form or another, almost given motives; they are seen in human terms. To do this, we don't need to falsify anything, but rather we highlight a particular way of seeing it – because this is precisely the way students' imaginations are engaged by knowledge.

Imaginative Education helps us with our lesson planning. It helps us to harness the power of naturally occurring ways of thinking by imbuing our topics with these. It gives us sets of questions to consider before we even start work on the practical preparation of our lessons. This way of working doesn't just wake our students up – it wakes us up too by helping us to rethink what we teach and how we teach it.

(You can find many more examples of how you can use single cognitive tools in the Teachers Tips section of the IERG website, http://ierg.net/lessonplans/cognitive_tools.php.)

3.1 Exploratory talk ground rules

> Exploratory talk

Focus: Encouraging students to understand what makes a good learning conversation. Setting up ground rules for later lessons. Speaking and listening.

Level: Pre-Intermediate upwards

Time: 20 minutes

Materials/Preparation: None.

in class

1. Introduce the idea that people can use conversation to help each other to think and learn. Use a simple example that has happened in class recently or that has happened to you, e.g. talking over a problem or decision with a friend so that you came up with some new insights. Ask students if this sort of thing sometimes happens to them too. Let them tell you about it.

2. Ask them what sorts of things can help to make a conversation useful for thinking and learning. Start off with an example of your own such as 'You need to listen really carefully to each other'. Write this up on a poster or other long-term display area.

3. As students come up with ideas, listen to them carefully, ask them why they think these things are important and listen to their reasons. In other words, have an exploratory talk with them. As ideas emerge and are refined, write them up. Continue until you have covered the following important features of exploratory talk:
   - talk one at a time
   - share ideas
   - question ideas
   - give reasons
   - consider
   - involve everybody
   - respect other people's opinions
   - accept responsibility for what you say
   - if we disagree, ask 'Why?'
   - try to agree in the end.

4. You now have a framework for the future, so keep this visible in the classroom or encourage each student to make their own copy and keep it handy.

Follow-up / Variations
Until students are used to it, whenever you want to work on exploratory talk, ask students to review first what it is for and then the ground rules you have all come up with.

3.2 Gathering exploratory talk language

> Exploratory talk

Focus: Teaching students the English for engaging in exploratory talk without lapsing into mother tongue (see target language below).

Level: Pre-Intermediate upwards

Time: 10 minutes for each set of phrases below. Do this activity after you have completed activity 3.1.

Materials/Preparation: Think through the ground rules from activity 3.1 and gather the target language phrases that they imply for your level of students. See below for examples.

in class

1. Elicit from students the purpose of exploratory talk and the ground rules you all came up with in the earlier lesson.

2. Explain that, little by little, they will be learning the English they need to do exploratory talk. Then take the ground rules, one by one, and elicit and teach phrases suitable for their level in your normal way. Low-level examples are:
    Sharing ideas: What do *you* think? I think …
    Listening carefully: Mmm, that's interesting. Tell me more …?
      What did X just say?
    Questioning ideas: Why do you think that?
    Giving reasons: Because … if …
    Involving everybody: What do *you* think, X?
    Considering: But what about …?
    Disagreeing: I'm not sure about that!
    Agreeing: I agree.
    Respecting others' opinions: I see. I understand your point.
    One at a time: Ssssh! X is talking. I can't hear!

3. Store the language somewhere publicly or be sure that all students have access to their own copy. Leave space under each category so that more phrases can be added.

Follow-up / Variations
Next time you want to work with exploratory talk, you can review its uses and ground rules (see TT4 and activity 3.1) and also the language of exploratory talk that you have taught students.

3.3 Doing exploratory talk

> Exploratory talk

Focus: Helping students to explore ideas by talking together. Speaking and listening.

Level: Pre-Intermediate upwards

Time: 30 minutes

Materials/Preparation: Make sure you have done the work on ground rules and useful phrases in activities 3.1 and 3.2 above. Choose a problem situation that will interest your students.

in class

1. Remind students of the point of exploratory talk and of its ground rules.

2. Review useful language for exploratory talk.

3. Give students a problem to work on in groups. Mercer (2000) offers a sample problem called 'The Dog's Home'. Students have one list of different types of dogs (breed, size, age, sex, habits, personalities) and another list of families (number of people, ages of any children, work patterns, type of house they live in etc).

4. Explain that the idea is to have a conversation to try to find which dog will suit which family of owners. There will be many possible permutations. The idea is not to come up with one fast right answer, but to explore together in conversation all the different aspects to consider. Give a time limit and have students begin.

5. In plenary, ask students what they talked about. Use exploratory talk yourself, i.e. listen well, ask students for reasons etc.

6. Next, refer back to the ground rules and ask which ones the groups feel they did well and which ones they will need to work on a bit harder next time.

Follow-up / Variations
Next time you practise exploratory talk, remind students of which ground rules they felt they needed to work harder on.

3.4 Inspiring people

> Associating with our heroes

Focus: Research, reading and writing. Making a personal association with someone who has overcome difficulties or achieved great things.

Level: Intermediate

Time: 25 minutes plus homework

Materials/Preparation: Information about a personal hero of yours, including perhaps a short biography, a picture and some quotations. Add the names of others who have made a substantial contribution to society, together with a little basic information about each one (see step 2 and the Note for suggestions). Make a handout from your list. Optional: prepare the questions in step 4 for display. Students will need access to the internet to do the homework research.

in class

1. Introduce the topic of *Inspiring People* by giving the name of somebody that you yourself admire. This person should not be a relative and can be from the world of music, community work, sport, politics, engineering, or science, for example. Encourage students to ask you questions about who the person is/was, where they live(d) and what they do/did that makes you admire them.

2. Explain that you are going to give them the names of some inspiring people so that they too can choose one person to find out about. Hand out names that represent a good mixture of women and men, different ages, continents of origin and spheres of excellence. Give students a little information about each one, for example 'Shirin Ibadi won the Nobel peace prize in 2003. She is from Iran.' 'Rosa Parks lived in the USA. She is famous for being on a bus!'

3. Students choose one of the people, or if they are unsure who to choose, give them one name each. If you have a large class, let students work in pairs or threes on this with others who are interested in or who have been given the same person.

4. Write up the following questions on the board or display them, and ask students to copy them. These will form the basis of their homework research into their inspiring person.

3.4 Inspiring people

Researching an inspiring person

Can you find a picture of your person? (via Google Images, for example, though remember to check for any copyright restrictions)

Can you find out when and where the person lived and something about their life?

What are they most famous for?

Can you find a quotation of something they said?

What do you find to admire about this person?

In what ways are you the same as this person?

For homework, each student or pair/trio of students researches into their person and writes a paragraph as a result.

Follow-up
Students can be asked to give short talks about their inspiring person to other students. Alternatively their texts and pictures can be collected into a class folder called *Inspiring People* or *Our Heroes*.

Variations
Students can choose their own hero to research into and to write and talk about. They may learn more, however, if they are asked by you to research someone outside their normal sphere of interest.

Note
For some people you could include in your list, try searching the internet for *Time 100 heroes and icons*, *Sporting heroes*, *Musical heroes*, *Winner Nobel peace prize* etc, and visit www.biographyonline.net.

Behold the humble button!

> Associating with our heroes

Focus: Speaking, listening and writing. Vocabulary development. Describing objects and processes. The language of comparatives.

Level: Intermediate

Time: 30 minutes

Materials/Preparation: You need a large collection of different buttons. You need to decide on useful target vocabulary for the activity; for some ideas, see step 1.

in class

1. Show a few buttons to the class and encourage them to look at any they may be wearing. Then work on related vocabulary; write up on the board the words that you can elicit or teach in categories with short starter phrases thus:

It's ...
  Size, e.g. *small, tiny*
  Shape, e.g. *round, square, irregular*
  Material, e.g. *glass, plastic, wooden*
It's got ...
  Parts, e.g. *rim, holes, surface, back*
It's quite / very /...
  Features, e.g. *shiny, dull*
It's also got ...
  Marks, e.g. *scratch, dent, broken corner.*

---

2. Ask students how buttons are made, where you buy them on their own, how else you get them, what you do with them, and what can happen to them. Write up any useful words and phrases as you go along.

3.5 Behold the humble button!

3. Next, pour out all your buttons in a pile or piles somewhere students can see them. Ask students to walk silently to the buttons, to choose one that they like, and to take it back to their desks and examine it very carefully.

4. Ask students to write a sentence or two describing their personal button, using the first set of words on the board and in the order of the categories on the board. This will mean their adjective order is correct. Help any students wanting new words, for example *metallic* or *rectangular*.

5. Ask a few students to read out what they have.

6. Ask students to imagine the life story of their personal button. Where was the button 'born'? What was its early life like? What was a high point in its life? A low point? What are its hopes and dreams now? Give students a few minutes to think about what they are going to say and to make a few notes and ask you for any words they want. Then, in pairs, they tell their button's life story to a partner.

7. Finally, ask students to consider in what ways they are the same as and different from their personal button. Ask them to tell their partner, and then write a few sentences for homework about that.

8. Gently separate your students from their buttons so that you can retain your collection!

Follow-up
In the next lesson, ask students to give in their sentences for correction or ask students to read out their ideas.

Variations
Instead of buttons, you can use any collection of objects that is cheap, easily accessible and transportable. I have had good results with apples and potatoes. The good thing about using fruit and vegetables is that students can take them home after class for fun, to help them with their homework and to eat!

CHAPTER 4
USING EVERYDAY THINKING FRAMEWORKS

In everyday life we use lots of thinking frameworks to help us sort out our thoughts on different issues. For example, we might sit down and make a list of all the advantages and disadvantages of relocating to a new city before making a decision about whether to make the move. We might come up with informal categories when sorting all the odd stuff in the garage for more organised storage or for sale.
We can use any of these everyday ways of thinking in language lessons.[1] In this chapter, we will play with two everyday thinking frameworks that encourage mental exercise. The first is listing. The second is reversals.

---

1   *If you like the idea of using simple, everyday thinking frameworks with your class for interesting language development, then have a look at Woodward (2006).*

Teaching Tips

TT1 **Listing**

Many language learners already use and encounter lists a lot. There are the three-column lists found at the back of course books laying out the Base form, Past Simple form and Past Participle of irregular verbs (e.g. *go, went, gone*). Then there are the lists students often like to keep when learning new words (e.g. *Pferde = horse*). As lists are easy to make and understand and familiar to everyone, listing is a good thinking framework to start playing with.

Making a list involves choosing a topic, searching our knowledge and memory store for related items, pulling these things out, recording them, often one under the other, often unprioritised, and noticing them one by one.

About lists generally, you might find the following useful:
- www.sixthings.net, a blog project by Lindsay Clandfield, which is a miscellany of English language teaching in list form and may inspire you with other ideas for using lists for or with your students. For example, it contains reference to the six most frequent collocations in English and a list of six tips for setting homework.
- www.listverse.com, which is a website dedicated to lists of trivia from a variety of categories – one of the most popular of which is lists of misconceptions (see activity 4.3)

There is also a written short story which is composed entirely of lists (see 'Lists' by Michele Roberts in *Playing Sardines* Virago, 2002).

TT2 **Reversals**

If we were to use a metaphor for thinking, such as *thinking is movement* – for we do talk about *moving ahead with an idea* – then to be truly flexible and strong in our thinking we should be able to move backwards as well as forwards. Sometimes it's only when we *slam on the brakes*, *go into reverse*, *do a U turn*, or *meet a paradox* that we break free from reproductive non-thinking and move into more productive thinking. We just have to think about the unusualness of, e.g., wearing our watch upside down for a day or two, or turning something upside down to draw it better, or making a room plan by looking up at the ceiling instead of looking at the floor, to see the potential interest and surprise of reversing things.

As language teachers, we already employ partial reversal techniques such as when we ask students to rewrite stories that they have become familiar with by changing the ending, the genders, the times and tenses, the overall tone from factual to romantic, or the genre

Teaching Tips

from poem to newspaper article. Just for fun, we may occasionally ask students to spell a word backwards. We may ask students to list the objects they would not want to have in their house or not take on holiday with them, and to tell us why. We can ask students to present themselves to each other by what they have not got, don't do and are not (e.g. 'I haven't got an iPod', 'I don't wear much make up' and 'I'm not greedy'). In activity 4.7 onwards are some more ideas for encouraging students to reverse other things.

4.1 Rules for a good society

> Listing

Focus: Encouraging students to recognise the part lists play in life. Connected vocabulary and structures such as *do ...*, *don't ...* .

Level: Pre-Intermediate upwards

Time: 30 minutes

Materials/Preparation: A list of the school rules (see below for other possibilities).

in class

1. Ask students how they or their parents remember what to buy when they go shopping. Do they look at a list on the fridge before they go, or take a list on a piece of paper with them?

2. Elicit from students other times when they, family or friends plan by making lists, e.g. before a holiday of what to pack and take, before a party of what food and drink and decorations to buy, before the week starts, when writing down experiences prior to a job application or college interview, when drawing up an agenda for a meeting, when writing letters to Father Christmas, when remembering past girlfriends or boyfriends, when thinking what CDs they own ... whatever is within the likely experience of your group.

3. Help with connected vocabulary such as *to make a list*, *to write things up / down*, *to tick / cross things off*, *a CV*, *to take stock*, *New Year's resolutions* and *Christmas lists*, as these words and phrases come up.

4. Next, remind the class that there are public lists too, such as passenger lists on planes and lists of guests at a hotel. Then take a list well known to your students, such as the list of school rules. Before displaying the whole list to the group or before telling them the name of the list, read out some items and have people guess the title of the list.

5. Once students have guessed the title of the list or you have told them, show them a copy of the list of rules and lead a brief discussion of what the list is for.

6. Invite students each to write a similar list of their own. It should contain, say, five to ten essential behaviours for modern life.

4.1 Rules for a good society

Students can write trivial things like *Don't switch TV programmes over without asking your friends what they want to see* or non-trivial such as *Don't tell lies*. Help students with vocabulary as they work.

7. In pairs or groups, students read their lists out. You can help them with list intonation (up, up, up and finally down). You can then discuss the interesting ones, laugh at the amusing ones and, if appropriate, discuss what makes social groups work well.

Follow-up / Variations
You can vary the topic: instead of asking students to write lists of essential social behaviours as in the main activity, and depending on which sort of list you first share with them, you can ask them to write their top ten list of hit singles, their favourite films of the year, their favourite places to visit, their top ten target words of the year, their favourite music of all time (their own Desert Island Discs), or the top ten things they would put in their shopping basket and so on.

You can vary the procedure; instead of reading out the items and asking students to guess the title of the list, give the title of a prioritised list and read out the items, but have people guess in which order the items appear. Alternatively, ask students to re-order jumbled versions of a prioritised list. This work will naturally throw up opinions language, ordinals, comparatives and superlatives (e.g. 'No way is that first or better', 'I think this is much more important', 'Right! I agree. That's about the same').

4.2 I'm grateful for …

> Listing

Focus: Thinking about life from a positive point of view. Vocabulary development.

Level: Elementary upwards

Time: 10 minutes

Materials/Preparation: None.

in class

1. Ask students to think back over the last five days and to write down five things in their lives for which they feel thankful. This can be done in class or for homework. As you will want them to share at least some of these things out loud in class later, alert students to this.

2. Once students have had time to compile their lists, and they have been checked for language support, ask students to read out some of the items. This can be done in different ways, e.g. you can pick the lists up, read out one list anonymously and students guess whose list it is. Or students read out one item each around the class. If these single items are written up on the board, students then come up with categories for the items, e.g. *Home, Friendships, Family, Health, Successes* or whatever categories seem to fit the items best.

Follow-up / Variations
A productive, 'feel good' variation is to ask students to write ten things that make them feel happy. Each sentence is to start with *I feel happy when …* (see activity 4.6 to make this into a list poem).

Acknowledgement
I first read about the health and happiness effects of listing things for which we feel grateful in Zimbardo and Boyd (2008, p. 88).

4.3 True or false *or* Facts and myths

> Listing

Focus: Speaking and listening. Discussion language. Practice of Present Simple.

Level: Intermediate upwards

Time: 30 minutes

Materials/Preparation: You need a list of ten well-known or fascinating beliefs or myths that are wrong. You can get a list such as this from the internet (search for 'the 20 greatest historical myths' or 'top ten fascinating facts that are wrong'). Choose ones that are of interest to your class. Many items will feature the Present Simple tense as they are about things which are generally thought to be true.

in class

1. Tell the class you will dictate four or five things that most people think are true. Your students should write them down.

2. Depending on the interests of your group, you then read out 'facts' such as 'one dog year is equal to seven human years' or 'lifts can kill when their cable snaps' or 'spinach makes you strong' or 'St Bernard dogs carry flasks of brandy round their necks'. Students write the sentences down.

3. Next, ask students to discuss in pairs or small groups whether they think the statements are true or false and why they think so. They should record their verdict each time. Allow a clear time limit of, say, 10 minutes.

4. Once students have had time to discuss the facts and record their verdicts, encourage open discussion. After each fact has been discussed, reveal the truth. You can do this by handing out a text, reading it out or simply telling the class what you know.

Follow-up / Variations
Students can go on to find well known myths themselves by doing research on the internet. They can then take it in turns to present their topic to the class.

4.4 How times have changed!

> Listing

Focus: Speaking and listening. Practice of Past Simple, *used to*, Present Perfect and Present Simple tenses. Vocabulary development.

Level: Intermediate

Time: 20 minutes

Materials/Preparation: A list of typical products bought by ordinary people in a past year (see below).

in class

1. Give students a short list such as the one below for 1947 from the UK Office of National Statistics. This can be on the board or on a handout.

> **Typical products bought in 1947**
> Wild rabbits
> Tinned milk
> Coal
> Clothes mangle
> Tin kettle
> Boy's two-piece suit
> Girl's slip *(petticoat)*
> Motorbike licence
> Radio licence
> Gramophone record

2. Work through the list explaining in your usual way any items that students do not know.

3. Ask students why they think people in 1947 bought those products. This will bring up vocabulary such as, *ready-made meals, supermarkets, central heating, formal dress*. Help students to create utterances with *used to* and Past Simple as in, 'People didn't have electric kettles then. They used to boil kettles on the cooker or on the fire.'

4.4 How times have changed!

4. Ask students how life is different for us now. Help students to make sentences such as *Nowadays we don't need to ... because we have ...* or *These days we can't ... because we ...*

5. Ask students how they think life has changed overall between then and now. Students may say, for example, 'Making meals has got easier. Doing the washing has got quicker' or 'We don't get as much exercise now'.

Follow-up
Ask students to talk to their parents or grandparents about life in the past. They can then bring notes in for a class discussion another day or write a short paragraph about what they have found out.

Notes
For lists of typical products bought in more recent years in the UK, search the internet for the Office for National Statistics shopping basket 2000 (or any other recent year).

4.5 Are we the same or different?

> Listing

Focus: Reading, writing, speaking and listening. Vocabulary development. The language of comparison.

Level: Pre-Intermediate upwards

Time: Lesson 1: 10 minutes
Lesson 2: 20 minutes

Materials/Preparation: Pictures to stimulate interest in a destination (for step 1). Web site addresses, texts or short video clips for student research. For Lesson 2, draw up the 'to do' and 'to take' lists that you would make before going off on a trip.

in class

Lesson 1

1. Ask students to imagine that they are going on a trip to Sydney (or London or New York depending what fits in with their interests and the topics in your course book). Raise interest in the topic by showing some visuals.

2. Explain that for homework, they need to do a little research into the destination so that they can make a list of all the things they could plan to do before they go and things they could take with them for this fantasy one-week trip. Give a couple of examples such as, *charge my mobile phone, take my camera*. They will also need to decide on reasons for choosing the things they think they actually would do and actually would take.

3. Give the students a text or list of web sites for their homework research.

Lesson 2

4. Once the homework is in, corrected and handed back, remind students of the comparative structures they know.

4.5 Are we the same or different?

5. Show students your own two trip lists.

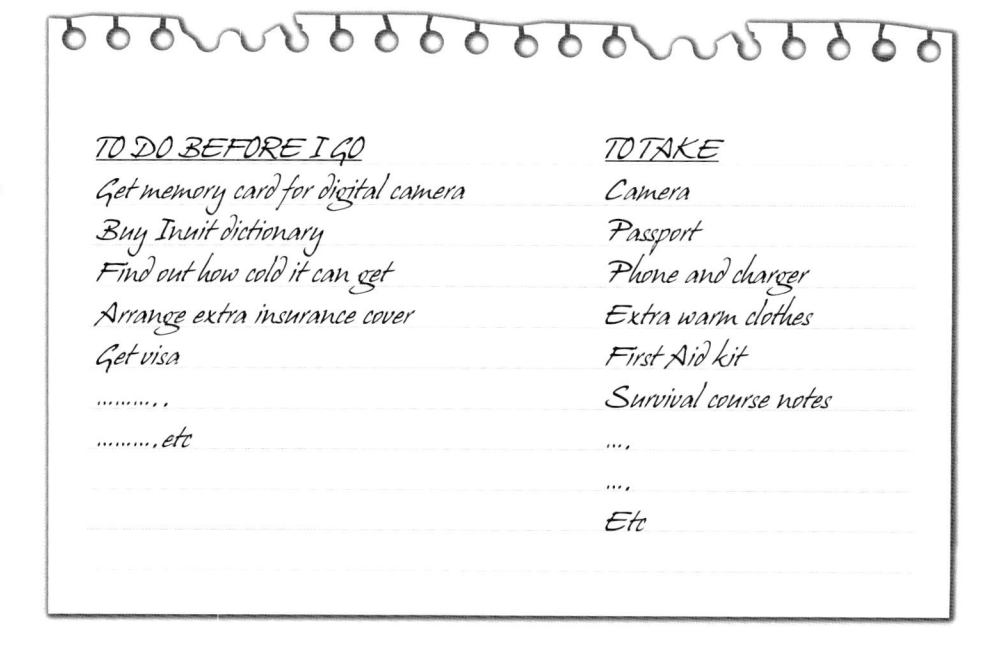

> TO DO BEFORE I GO
> Get memory card for digital camera
> Buy Inuit dictionary
> Find out how cold it can get
> Arrange extra insurance cover
> Get visa
> ....,,
> ....,etc
>
> TO TAKE
> Camera
> Passport
> Phone and charger
> Extra warm clothes
> First Aid kit
> Survival course notes
> ....,
> ....,
> Etc

6. Talk about the similarities and differences between the 'to do' and 'to take' lists and the criteria behind the choices. Then ask them to compare their trip lists in groups of three and to see in what ways they are the same and different both in items and in the reasons or criteria used for choosing the items. They need to talk this over and then produce three different sentences each about the comparisons.

7. The sentences can be taken in and corrected or some read out loud. The class can then vote on the best criteria for choosing.

Follow-up
Ask students what can be learned about a person from listening to or reading their 'to do' and 'to take' lists. When students come up with an idea, ask them to support it with a real example from the three lists they looked at in their groups.

4.6 List poems

> Listing

Focus: Writing and reading. Grammatical structure depending on the poem frame (see below).

Level: Elementary upwards

Time: 20 minutes

Materials/Preparation: You need the list poem below for students to read.

in class

1. Give students the list poem to read, and help them to understand it.

> **I love it when** ...
> I love it when people smile at me.
> I love it when music starts to play.
> I love it when dinner is ready.
> I love it when there is a sunny spot in the garden.
> I love it then. I love it then.

2. Ask students to write the title on a piece of paper and then to write four sentences starting with *I love it when* ... The sentences should be different from the ones in the poem above, and should be true about them. They should finish the poem with the final line as above.

3. Go around helping students with vocabulary and, if necessary, ideas.

4. When most students are ready, ask those who want to, to read their poems out loud.

Variations
A Texts can be taken in, corrected and then read out loud by you while students try to guess who wrote them.

B The poems can be displayed on a wall or collected on a class web page. Students can then read each other's poems.

4.6 List poems

C Any poem that has a title, a repeated grammatical structure and an ending can be used. There are many list poem sites on the internet. These could be interesting for students to read.

D Other possible topics are: *My brother/sister drives me crazy when s/he ...*, *My best friend never ...*, *Something I find interesting is ...* .

Acknowledgement
I first learned about list poems from Tsai and Feher (2004).

4.7 Right name wrong name

> Reversals

Focus: Speaking and listening. Vocabulary.

Level: Elementary upwards

Time: 10 minutes

Materials/Preparation: None.

in class

1. Explain that there are two parts to the activity. In pairs, in the first part, one person will point to something in the room and name it in English, e.g. person A points to the wall and says 'Wall!' If B thinks the word is right, they simply agree and say, 'Yes. Wall!' Set a time limit of one or two minutes and ask pairs to go ahead taking it in turns to point and name or to agree.

2. In this phase you may need to help out students who do not agree on a word or who point to something they want to know the name of in English.

3. Once students have done this for a couple of minutes, ask them to stop. Write on the board any words they asked you about during the pair work.

4. Next, explain that in part two of the activity they will stay in the same pairs. Again they take it in turns to point to something in the room, but this time they must label the object *wrongly*. Give them an example by, e.g., pointing to the ceiling and saying, 'Floor!' or to the door and saying, 'Prison!' The other person in the pair this time simply repeats the wrong word. Set a time limit of a few minutes and let students start.

5. Enjoy the laughter during this phase, and if there is anything particularly funny (such as students pointing at the teacher and saying, 'Crocodile!') share it with the class afterwards.

6. Work on any vocabulary students need as before.

Acknowledgement
I learned the power of reversals activities from Johnstone (1981).

4.8 That's not right! *or* 'Cinderfella'

> Reversals

Focus: Listening to a story and correcting the teacher.

Level: Pre-Intermediate upwards

Time: 20 minutes

Materials/Preparation: Choose a story that you think your group will know well, and then prepare to tell it with lots of the details changed (see below).

in class

1. Explain to the class that you are going to tell them a story that you think they know well. The problem is that you haven't told it for a while so you can't remember it very clearly. They will need to listen and correct you when you go wrong, by saying, 'No, that's wrong!' and helping you to say what is right.

2. Start off with a well-known tale such as Cinderella (or Red Riding Hood or a well-known local folk tale), but say the name of the story wrong, e.g. 'This is a story about a girl called … hmmm … can I remember it right? *Cinderfella*, I think.' Wait for students to call out, 'No, that's wrong!' Ask them to correct you, and someone will say *Cinderella*. 'Oh yes, I remember now!' you say. 'Yes, that's right. There was once a girl called Cinderella!'

3. You gradually go on telling the story but getting basic details wrong, e.g. you say that she had three lovely sisters or she was happy. She lived upstairs with the family. She could play all day. Before each deliberate mistake look doubtful and pretend you can't remember the story very well. Once you have been corrected, loop back to include the correct details.

4. Once the correct story is out, you can congratulate the class on having a better memory than you. Then ask them in pairs to help each other to reconstruct the story from memory. They can say it or write it, as you prefer. They can reconstruct the corrected version or, if you or they prefer, a rather different version based on your mistakes or other ideas.

Variation
Draw a line across the board and ask students to call out so that you can write up the main events in a familiar story such as Cinderella at points along the line. At each main point, draw a line leading away

4.8 That's not right! or 'Cinderfella'

from the main line. Discuss with students alternative possibilities, such as that Cinderella gets an invitation to attend two different parties or that she doesn't like Prince Charming. Discuss the possible alternative stories and how they might affect the ending.

Acknowledgement
I learned the variation from Bowker (2007).

4.9 Reversals anecdotes

> Reversals

Focus: Listening, mentally reversing details, then telling anecdotes with the details reversed.

Level: Pre-Intermediate upwards

Time: 20 minutes

Materials/Preparation: You need to tell a true story about something moderately awful but interesting that has happened to you. Prepare to tell it with the details reversed (see below).

in class

1. Explain to your class that you want to tell them about something that happened to you once. Explain that you are a bit shy or embarrassed about telling it so you are going to 'oppositise' all the details. They will have to listen and guess what really happened to you.
   Give a little example to start with, e.g. if telling them about an awful job you had once, you could say, 'I once had a really wonderful job!' Then stop and laugh or look uncertain. Ask students to guess the truth. Wait until one of them says 'Was it a bad job?' Agree and say that is how you will go on, telling the opposite of the truth. Ask them not to shout out what they think is true, but just to remember the details so they can talk about them later when you have finished your story.

2. Tell your anecdote slowly and reverse all the details. So if the job was in a cold country called Sweden, tell the class it was in a hot country called Sudan and so on. Pause significantly after all the wrong bits to give students time to think.

3. Once you have finished the anecdote, ask students in pairs to tell each other what they think really happened.

4. Next, students can ask you any questions they like about your anecdote to make sure they have got the real facts right.

5. Next, either for homework or in class, ask students to think of an unusual time in their lives when something either good or bad happened to them. It could be a great holiday or a failed exam. Ask them to prepare to tell people about it with many of the details reversed or 'oppositised'!

4.9 Reversals anecdotes

6. When students are ready, they can tell their anecdotes in pairs or groups, or write them down as an entry in a class 'Opposites' blog. However their anecdote is presented, the others in the class have to guess what really happened and then ask questions until the truth is out.

4.10 Working backwards from goals

> Reversals

Focus: Planning realistic aims and working out how to reach them. The language of planning, e.g. first conditional: *If I want to do X by Y, I will need to do Z.*

Level: Pre-Intermediate upwards

Time: 20 minutes

Materials/Preparation: None.

in class

1. Ask students to look forward to something that they wish to achieve in English. This could be a class goal such as passing a particular school or public exam. Or it could be a personal goal such as finishing a whole graded reader or learning 100 new words in English or being able to write an email to a friend or colleague abroad in English or learning the words to an English song. They also need to write down a deadline by which they want to achieve their goal. Discuss the sorts of things they would like to achieve. If you have a class that works quickly, ask them to write down a few goals each now. If your class needs more thinking time, ask them to write down three goals for homework and then continue with steps 2-6 in a follow-up lesson.

2. Once students have arrived at some things they would like to do, ask them to break each one down into small, doable sub-tasks. So a student might write down:
   I want to learn lots of words about my hobby. I can learn about five a week. I want to spell them, say them and know the meaning. Once I have learned five or more, I need to keep reviewing the old ones too, so I don't forget them.

3. Next, ask students to put the sub-tasks in order of priority or a logical or chronological order, and to write that down or to draw a ladder or set of steps and write the sub-tasks onto that.

4. Then students need to figure out how long it might take to do the sub-tasks and if they will need any materials or help.

5. Next, ask students to set realistic start and finish dates for each task. They should include the time needed to get hold of any materials they need or support or help they have to get. They need

4.10 Working backwards from goals

to adjust all the times so that they can meet their overall deadline. They write it all down.

6. Explain to students that now, instead of worrying about the daunting task of tackling a large task, they can get started on a small, practical, doable sub-task.

Follow-up
Allow time in class for students to tell you how they are getting on with their sub-tasks. Help them to see that if they tackle small practical sub-tasks, then bit by bit the bigger aims will tend to take care of themselves. This sort of work is especially likely to be helpful for young children who have ambitious aims such as wanting to be doctors or vets, but who have little family back-up and so absolutely no idea how to go about achieving their aims.

Acknowledgement
I first learned this idea from Rena Subotnik when she worked with gifted children in schools in the USA.

4.11 Fortunately, unfortunately

> Reversals

Focus: Listening and speaking. Spontaneous storytelling.

Level: Intermediate upwards

Time: 20 minutes

Materials/Preparation: None.

in class

1. Write up the words *fortunately* and *unfortunately* on the board. Check that students know what they mean. Ask students if they know any other words or phrases with the same meaning. Write these up on the board too. Examples are *sadly, happily, luckily, unluckily, the good thing is/was, the bad thing is/was* ...

2. Explain that you will give the class the first line of a story. Each person (or every second or fifth person if you have a large class) will continue the story by making up the next line. They must however start with one of the words or phrases on the board and follow its sense by following or changing the story line given them by the person before them.

3. Have a practice. Give the first line of a story, such as:
    On Saturday the weather was great.
    The next person can choose any word or phrase from the board and so could continue by saying, 'Luckily, there was no school so I went to my friend's house.' The next student may decide to reverse fortunes by saying, 'Unfortunately, she was out!'

4. Using the same starter sentence, let the students begin again. Let the story progress around the class. Anybody can help with ideas. Students or you can thus prompt by whispering, e.g., 'Rain!' or 'No money!' or 'Cake!' so that nobody gets stuck for something to say.

Variations

A Other story starter sentences are:
  I was at home last night.
  My friend went on holiday last summer.
  I want my mum to get a dog.

4.11 Fortunately, unfortunately

B At higher levels, revise some connectors meaning *and* (such as *also, too, and another thing, we could also say*), and some meaning *but* (such as *while, whereas, but on the other hand*), and do the activity alternating these.

4.12 Change the text

> Reversals

Focus: Reading. Adjectives.

Level: Intermediate upwards

Time: 20 minutes

Materials/Preparation: A short text with plenty of adjectives in it (see below).

in class

1. Give the students a text such as:

   > Cindy is young and beautiful. She is also a famous model. She does TV adverts for hand cream. This means she has to keep her skin soft. So every night she puts rich, expensive cream on her lovely hands and goes to sleep with rubber gloves on.

2. Make sure students understand the text. Then ask them to underline all the adjectives in it.

3. Next, individually, students rewrite the text changing all the adjectives to other words or phrases that have a different meaning. Thus, instead of writing *Cindy is young*, and depending on their level of English, they could write *Cindy is a teenager/in her thirties/88 years old*. They will end up with a written text with a very different feel to it.

4. Ask a few students to read out their texts and to explain their changes. So, for example, a student could say, 'Cindy is 90. She is not very famous. She does adverts for a special company. It wants to show older women as beautiful!' Enjoy the changes.

Variations
A Instead of reversing the meaning of adjectives, students could be asked to change the gender, the adverbs, or the time, using different texts.

4.12 Change the text

B Discuss with students adjectives that would diminish a person or an idea, words like *little, small, unimportant, disappointing, not very clever, old-fashioned*. Also elicit adjectives that would make something seem grand and good, such as *fabulous, huge, clever, triumphant*. Contrast this with neutral texts that do not generally have value judgements associated with them. These might be texts with few adjectives at all, or with words like *medium-sized* in them. Then let them loose writing two different short texts describing the same person, perhaps a sports personality or an actor. One text pumps the person up, the other diminishes them. Finally, help your students to construct a neutral text.

Acknowledgement
I first learned this technique from Spencer (1967). The idea for the text above came from Penny Ur.

4.13 Flip it and see

> Reversals

Focus: Speaking. Present Simple. Vocabulary development.

Level: Intermediate upwards

Time: 30 minutes

Materials/Preparation: Think up an unusual two-noun object for step 4.

in class

1. Write up a list on the board of two-word objects and devices such as these:

   ```
   Fridge magnet          CD player
   Tree house             Cuckoo clock
   Coal shed              Guitar string
   Traffic light          Bike lock
   Car park               Book mark
   Picture hook           Lamp post
   Garden fence           Summer dress
   ```

2. Check that students can tell you what they all are and what they are for.

3. Ask students to write a list of new objects by recombining the words or reversing or changing the order of the first and second words. So, for example, *string guitar*, *fridge mark*, *tree lock*, or *coal park*.

4. Talk about your own example and say what this newly-made device could be. So, for example, 'I've got a *fridge player*. This is a special new device that means every time I open the fridge, music plays. I can choose the music just like I can choose the ring tone on my mobile phone!'

4.13 Flip it and see

5. Ask students, alone or in pairs, to prepare to talk about some of the new devices they have come up with.

6. When ready they can share these out loud in the class.

Acknowledgement
This idea is based on Bowker (2007, p. 109).

CHAPTER 5
CREATIVE THINKING

We have a tendency perhaps to think that people who are very creative are just born that way. If we were not born geniuses or prodigies, then we might think that we are doomed to be non-creative and ordinary all our lives. But we were not born instant marathon runners or skilled teachers or gifted nurses either. And some of us have become so.

Perhaps we shouldn't look at creativity, then, as being an all-or-nothing gift. After all, we only have to look at an early sketch by, say, Vincent van Gogh and then contrast it with any of his later work to see what huge improvements a person can make if they put in the hundreds of hours of practice time necessary for real skill development. (To check this out for yourself, try an internet search for 'van Gogh The Carpenter', which is a rather rough, out-of-proportion, early sketch, and then compare this with any of his later work, from 1882 onwards.)

I believe we can get better at being creative just as we can get better at running than we were when we were young. But how can we practise 'being creative'? It seems a bit difficult. Luckily, however, there are many writers who have outlined techniques and principles to help us do just that.

In the first part of this chapter I'll take four principles underlying creativity that are often cited (e.g. Michalko, 1998) and which we can work on ourselves and with our students:
- be prolific
- use unusual or novel combinations
- make thinking visible, and
- use generative frameworks.

We have already had some examples of the use of unusual combinations to support the raising of a large number of interesting ideas (see activities 2.1, 2.10 and 4.13). In the final part of this chapter we will look at a very special kind of creativity, the ability to empathise with others.

Teaching Tips

TT1 Being prolific

If we don't get into the *habit* of producing plenty of work (without blocking ourselves by worrying that it isn't perfect), we will never feel able to put in the hours of skill practice we need to get better at anything we do. So, let's not always worry about the total accuracy of the communication that our students produce, but instead primarily encourage them to produce *plenty of work* and *plenty of different kinds of work*. Putting in time towards speaking fluently or writing, for example, is one way that students will get better at these skills. In activity 5.1 are some ideas that work towards this feeling of plethora, both in student work and in our own materials and techniques.

TT2 Creating unusual or novel combinations

With two or more things available to us and our students, whether these be real objects, pictures, texts or dialogues, ideas can begin to spark. By juxtaposing these things and forcing relationships between the apparently unconnected, we play at novel combinations and thus gain new results.

TT3 Making thinking visible

In our EFL classes we often use charts and tables, family tree diagrams, time lines, mind maps and many more graphic organisers. We use them because they can be fun, engaging and memorable and help us to think things through. They can point us to part to whole, chronological and other relationships, and can show students what they already know and what they have yet to learn. If we wish to encourage fresh thinking, then once students have been introduced to a useful visual or graphic organiser and have understood it, it is important for them to make one of their own rather than be given a ready-made, finished one. We have already used a Venn diagram (see activity 2.10). In activities 5.9–5.11 are some more ideas that help to make thinking visible. If a particularly useful graphic organiser is made or used in class, why not take a digital photo of it and post it on a blog or on your school web site?

TT4 Using generative frameworks

In chapter 4 we looked at simple everyday thinking frameworks such as listing and reversals. We looked at how they could be used for interesting mental exercise in EFL classes. In activities 5.12 and 5.13 there are some slightly more complex frameworks which once learned by students can help them to be very productive indeed.

Teaching Tips

TT5 **Building empathy**

Communicating with others in a foreign language can be fun and also very challenging. Attempting to be in tune with another person, trying to understand what they think and what their situation is like for them, is a special kind of imaginative leap which may help the communication endeavour. To encourage an empathetic mood in our classes, we can suggest that we all listen well to each other, set aside judgements, solutions and autobiographical responses, and summarise and paraphrase each other's contributions. From 5.15 onwards are activities that focus on building empathy and a feeling of connectedness between students.

5.1 Creativity brainstorm

> Being prolific

Focus: Students start to consider what they mean by *creativity*, and learn related vocabulary. Speaking and listening.

Level: Pre-Intermediate upwards

Time: 10 minutes

Materials/Preparation: None.

in class

1. Write the word *Creativity* in the middle of a large piece of poster paper and draw up to about 20 spokes radiating out from it.

2. Ask students to imagine a really creative film or a creative lesson or a very creative friend. Ask them what they would mean by that word. What is it that makes something or somebody creative? Give an example, e.g. 'Maybe we mean that there is something new or different from usual about the film or person?' Write the words *New*, *Different* and *Unusual* on the poster at the ends of three different spokes.

3. Wait until students venture a couple of other ideas. Accept them – 'Yes! Good idea!' – and write them up on the poster at the ends of new spokes.

4. Wait, accept, write all the suggestions up until you have a selection of words on the paper including ideas such as *movement, interesting visual, humour, fun, old things in new ways, colour, imagination, fast and slow, music, choice, challenging, surprising, intense, clever, relaxing, fantasy, play, experiments, makes you feel free, inventing*. Accept any words that have anything to do with creativity. Explain, translate or paraphrase any words that students have trouble with.

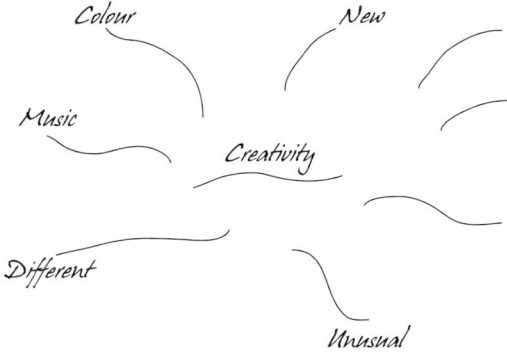

Colour   New
Music
Creativity
Different
Unusual

5.1 Creativity brainstorm

5. Ask students whether a film or book or video game or person would have to be *all* of these things at the same time to be creative. They will probably say not. Ask them if they would like it if in the lessons from now on, you and they and the lesson itself were just a little bit creative in one or more of these ways. Hopefully they will say, 'Yes!'

6. If possible, pin the poster up on the classroom wall so you can refer to it from time to time.

Follow-up / Variations

A Take a digital photo of the creativity display created and post it on a blog or on your school web site.

B From now on try to use a little colour or music or movement or a few pictures etc in your classes. When you manage to do so, at the end of the lesson you can point to the poster and ask students, 'If today we had anything a little bit creative in the lesson, which of the words would it be?' They can look at the poster spokes and say, e.g., 'We had coloured paper to do the writing on', or 'You drew a picture of the birds', or 'Movement! We were moving around to ask the questions!'

When you use a different element of creativity, ask students to look at the poster and say, 'What did we do today that was a bit creative and which is not written on the poster?' Give them hints, and when they say, e.g., 'We could really say what we wanted to! We could choose', or 'It was about us!' or 'The poem was nice!', write up new words and phrases at the end of new spokes, e.g. *Say what we want* or *Personal choice* or *Poems*.

5.2 You can use it to …

> Being prolific

Focus: Encouraging students to think past the obvious to get to the more creative and unusual. Using language such as *You can use it to …* and *You could use it for …ing*. Vocabulary development. Integrated skills.

Level: Pre-Intermediate upwards

Time: 15 minutes

Materials/Preparation: Bring in a simple everyday object.

in class

1. Invite students to look at a simple everyday object, such as a paper clip, that you have brought in. Elicit from students its normal use and write this up on the board, e.g. *You can use it to hold papers together* or *You can use it for holding papers together*. Point out these two useful ways of talking about an object's use.

2. Divide students into pairs or groups and ask them to write down a list of as many other things as possible they can think of that they could use the object for. Tell them the ideas can be as sensible or outlandish as they like. They do need to be possible, though. Mime an unusual example yourself and then say, e.g. 'You can use it to scratch an itch far down your back.' Give a time limit and say that later you will award points for ideas that make other people laugh or that are very unusual, or for the most ideas (or for whatever other criteria you wish).
Really unusual students might ask questions like 'Can the paperclip be 30 feet tall, pink and made of foam rubber?' You can decide if this is permissible or not.

3. While students are working, go round and help with vocabulary.

4. When the time is up, ask students to call out their ideas or, if you prefer, to write them on the board using the structures you wrote up earlier. Award points as previously stated.

Follow-up / Variations
You can use this idea with any everyday object, e.g. a brick, a metal coat hanger, a wooden spoon, or a bucket.

Acknowledgement
I first did this activity at an after-dinner speech given by Tony Buzan. I thoroughly enjoyed it!

5.3 Just one colour

> Being prolific

Focus: Helping students to notice details in their environment. Vocabulary development. Integrated skills.

Level: Elementary upwards

Time: 15 minutes

Materials/Preparation: Bring in a bell or whistle for step 1.

in class

1. Elicit from students the name of different colours. Ask them each to choose one they like and tell them that in a minute you will ask them to look around the room, out of the window, in their bags and, if this is possible in your setting, around the school corridors, for two minutes. At the end of two minutes, you will ring a bell or blow a whistle. During the two minutes they should write down the name of everything they see that is the colour they have chosen. Thus, if they choose red and they spot a red balloon in a picture on the classroom wall, they can write down *balloon.* They will get a point for every object they write down. If they are late back to their seat, they lose five points. If they don't know the name of something in English, they can write it down in mother tongue.

2. Set the students off and keep time. Once the time is up, make your pre-arranged signal and wait for students to settle down again.

3. Ask students to give you some examples of things they saw of their colour. Give individuals any English words they need. Ask them to learn these new words for homework.

Follow-up
Next time you see the students, ask them to read out their lists and count up all the words they have. Points can be given to those who have the longest lists, learned the most new words, noticed the most unusual things etc. You will need to be the judge of this last!

Variation
Change the criterion from colour to shape (e.g. square, round, spherical, rectangular, irregular shaped).

5.4 Thirty things I did

> Being prolific

Focus: Past Simple sentences involving everyday vocabulary. Pushing past the routine to the more unusual. Writing.

Level: Pre-Intermediate upwards

Time: 15 minutes

Materials/Preparation: None.

in class

1. Ask students to write 10 true sentences about what they did over the weekend or last night or during their holiday. If anybody complains and says, '10!?!' say, 'Not 10, then 20!' If students say '*20!!!*' say 'Oh, not 20, then 25!' Play the game until the students get the message that the number will go up if they keep complaining.

2. Explain that the reason why you want a lot of sentences is not just that it will give them lots of Past Simple practice but also that it will make them think about things they did which are not routine obvious answers but rather more unusual. This will be interesting for you to read and for them to recall.

Follow-up / Variations
Use the same basic strategy of going for large numbers of words, utterances or sentences, but change the topic. So, instead of asking students to come up with 30 things they did yesterday and upping the number every time students complain, you can ask for, e.g., 20 plans they have for the upcoming holidays, or 15 English words beginning with B, or 10 reasons why someone might not answer their phone, or 10 questions nobody would ask on a first date, or 100 reasons why students don't do their homework, or you could ask them to read 10 tiny texts from a 'news in brief' column in a newspaper.

5.5 Picture pack plethora

> Being prolific

Focus: Vocabulary. Speaking and writing.

Level: Pre-Intermediate upwards

Time: 20 minutes

Materials/Preparation:

1. So that students enjoy a feast of visuals, you need to collect a large number of pictures cut out from magazines, such as *National Geographic*, and calendars from around the world. Make sure the pictures show many different countries, climates, races of people, flora, fauna and objects.

2. For the students, you need a handout with sentences and sentence starters such as the one at the end of this activity, but adapted for your students' level.

3. Before class, or while students are busy with another activity, lay your pictures on tables around the room, spaced out so that students will be able to stroll around the room and look at them.

4. You may well need to have a good dictionary handy for yourself for step 2 or to have an internet dictionary such as www.onelook.com ready on a laptop.

in class

1. Ask students to walk around and find a picture that they like and to take it back to their desk.

2. Encourage them to search in a dictionary for words or to ask you for any words they will need later to describe their picture.

3. Explain to students that you'll ask them to do a short piece of writing or to talk for a while (whichever you prefer) about their picture, using a simple handout like the example to help them structure what they want to say.

4. Make sure every student has a copy of the handout, and encourage them to look at it while you talk about a picture you have chosen. Use the sentence starters on the handout.

5. Answer any questions students may have about your picture or the sentence starters, and give them time to prepare to talk or write about their own picture.

5.5 Picture pack plethora

6. Students in pairs then show each other their picture and explain why they chose it, like it, and so forth.

7. If you have time, students can show their picture to two or three different people, trying each time to talk more fluently and more fully about it.

Follow-up / Variations

1. In their pairs, students can put their two different pictures together and imagine some sort of connection between the two. Give them time to come up with a possible story line for the two pictures.

2. Next, ask them to walk around and look at the pictures left on the tables, now choosing one or two new ones that will support their joint story line.

3. Pairs sit together, fill out their story and then work out who will tell which part of it (if you use this as a speaking activity) or help each other to write the story.

4. Either in this lesson or the next, pairs then show their pictures to the rest of the class or to other pairs. Alternatively they can tell their story.

Example handout

> *Talking about a picture*
> This is the picture I chose.
> I chose it because …
> I especially like …
> Look! You can see …
> It reminds me of …
> It takes me back to …
> It makes me think of …
> If you look closely, you can see …
> I'm not sure …
> I wonder …
> I don't know …
> I'd like to know what this is in English.

5.6 Checking vocabulary many ways

> Being prolific

Focus: Giving students a variety of ways of checking vocabulary. This reminds them how much there is to know about a word (see activity 1.6).

Level: Elementary upwards

Time: 10 minutes

Materials/Preparation: Prepare a list of different ways that you can review or check new words and phrases that have come up during your lesson. See the possible list at the end of this activity.

in class

1. Teach your lesson in your usual way, making a note of any new words and phrases that come up.

2. Towards the end of the class or at the beginning of the next class, review the new vocabulary. Use a different checking method for each item, as far as possible. Have a list, such as the one below, near you as a reminder.

Follow-up / Variations
Once students have had exposure to many different ways of reviewing or checking vocabulary, for a useful warm-up or closing activity they can use these techniques themselves when they test each other in pairs.

Ways to review or check new words and phrases
The meaning of this word is ... So what's the word?
Give me a word which means the same as ...
Give me a word that means the opposite of ...
Please spell this word backwards ...
Look at the word on the board and clap the stress pattern
(see activity 2.8.)
Look at the word on the board and step out the stress pattern with your fingers.
Please give me an example of this word.
This is the word. What does it mean?
What words often go with this word?
What word class is it?
Here is a mime / gesture / noise / picture. What's the word?
This is a place where ... / This is a person who ... / This is a thing that ... So, what's the word?
Look at the sentence on the board. What word goes in the gap?

5.7 Comparing a text and a picture

> Using unusual or novel combinations

Focus: Getting to know a text well and then even better by comparing it to a seemingly unrelated picture. Language development depends on the picture (see Materials 2).

Level: Pre-Intermediate upwards

Time: 20 minutes

Materials/Preparation:

1. Select any interesting text, poem or song lyrics that you think students will enjoy, and make a copy for each student.

2. You also need a large, colourful visual. You could take one from your picture pack (see activity 5.5). Calendars are possible sources, as are large images or clip-arts from the internet, displayed (copyright permitting) via data projector. The picture does not need at first glance to have anything to do with the text.

in class

1. Work with the text in your usual way to make sure that students understand it and have a grasp of its vocabulary, style etc.

2. Next, place the picture where students can see it, and ask the students to look at it carefully.

3. Ask the students – individually or in pairs or trios – to come up with as many ways as they can in which the text and the picture are alike. Although at first glance the text and the picture will seem completely unrelated, the mind, being what it is, will search for some kind of connection in terms of colour, shape, number, emotion, topic, meaning etc.

4. Share the ideas among the whole class.

Follow-up / Variations

A Ask students to do one of the following:
   - Draw or find a different picture for the text. It does not have to represent the text at all. It can be completely unconnected.
   - Choose a different text and draw or find a picture (from a magazine or the internet) that they think could work well for this activity.

B Students can be asked to compare any two things that on the face of it seem to be unconnected, e.g. themselves and a soft toy, or an EFL class and a factory (see also activity 2.10).

5.8 If she were an animal, she'd be a panther!

> Using unusual or novel combinations

Focus: Introducing a person in an unusual way. Use of the second conditional. Speaking, listening and writing. Vocabulary development.

Level: Intermediate upwards

Time: 15 minutes

Materials/Preparation: Be prepared to talk about someone you know well in the unusual way described below.

in class

1. Tell the class you are going to describe someone you know well, for example a friend.

2. Tell them a little bit about the person, for example who they are, where and when you met, where they live etc.

3. Once you've covered the basics, start to talk about the person using the following sentence starters:
   If she was (or were) a vehicle, she would be a ...
   If she was an animal, she would be a ...
   If she was a colour, she would be a ...
   If she was a textile, she would be a ...
   If she was a perfume, she would be a ...
   If she was a sound, she would be a ...
   If she was a drink, she would be a ...

   For example:
   'If she was a vehicle, she would be a large, black Jaguar car with padded seats.'

   'If she was a colour, she would be a rich red.'

5.8 If she were an animal, she'd be a panther!

4. Once you have finished describing your friend, let students ask you any questions they like and encourage them to tell you what they feel they've learned about your friend.

5. Ask them if they can remember any of the things that you compared your friend to. As students call words out – e.g. *a vehicle* and *a jaguar*, or *a colour* and *red* – write these on the board.

6. Ask students to give examples to go under each of the superordinates, e.g. for *vehicle* they could give *bicycle, sports car, tractor, bike, roller skates, horse and cart*. At lower levels, write these words up on the board.

7. Ask students to think of somebody they know really well, to prepare to describe them in normal ways and then to use four or five of the unusual categories. If necessary, put one of your example sentences on the board, highlighting the use of the second conditional.

Follow-up / Variations
For homework, ask students to write a text describing someone they know well in this way, and to hand it in for correction.

Acknowledgement
I got this idea from Gerngross, Puchta and Thornbury (2006).

5.9 Scrabble word review

> Making thinking visible

Focus: Helping students to review a field of associated words. Integrated skills.

Level: Elementary upwards

Time: 10 minutes

Materials/Preparation: Keep a note of words you have taught on topics or themes. Work out a scrabble formation for the words, as in step 2.

in class

1. Tell the students you are going to review a group of words they have learned recently. Elicit the main topic word from them and write on the board, e.g. *What is the name for all the bones in our body?* The students may remember the word *skeleton* that you taught them, so write it on the board with plenty of space around it.

2. Elicit the connected words from the students and write them up in a scrabble formation. e.g.:

```
            C
            A         B
        S K E L E T O N
        U   C         N
        P   I         E
        P   U
        O   M
        R
        T
```

5.9 Scrabble word review

3. Students can copy the figure into their books.

Follow-up / Variations
Ask students to prepare a similar scrabble formation for another set of words on a different topic another time. They help other students to complete their own copy of it by asking questions, just as you did in class.

5.10 Musical post cards

> Making thinking visible

Focus: Capitalising on the capacity for daydreaming and using it to develop vocabulary and write texts.

Level: Pre-Intermediate upwards

Time: 20 minutes

Materials/Preparation: Atmospheric music (for step 4) and some blank postcards, one per student.

in class

1. Write the following list of words down the left-hand side of the board: *Geography* (or *Place*), *Climate* (or *Weather*), *Colours*, *Buildings*, *People*, *Animals*, *Plants*, *Events*, *Other*.

2. Explain that in a minute you will ask everybody to relax and to shut their eyes and listen to some music. Explain that, while listening, they will probably see pictures in their mind's eye. They might 'go' to a place. Any place is okay. They should let the music take them there and just notice what they see.

3. Elicit a few ideas under each category on the board, e.g. under *Geography* or *Place* students might offer *mountains*, *flat place* or *tundra*, depending on their level and knowledge of the world.

4. Ask the students to shut their eyes and then play them some instrumental world music. It could be flutes from Peru or drums from the Sahara or Japanese *shakohachi*. As long as it is very different from where they usually live, it will be fine. A couple of minutes of the music will be enough.

5. Turn the music down gradually and ask the students to come back to the room. Pair them, and ask them to tell their partners what they 'saw'. There is no right or wrong answer.

6. Next, ask several students what they saw and help them with any new words they need.

7. Give each student a blank postcard. Ask them to draw a representation of what they saw on one side. On the other side they write a message, as if from a trip to their place, to a friend.

5.10 Musical post cards

8. Once the fronts and backs of the post cards have been finished, either in class or for homework, they can be corrected and handed back or displayed on the wall.

Note
For more ideas that use the mind's eye for language work, see Arnold, Puchta and Rinvolucri (2007).

Acknowledgement
I learned step 7 from Andreas Tribus.

5.11 Graphic organiser variety

Making thinking visible

Focus: Using visual aids to help organise thoughts.

Level: Elementary upwards

Time: 10–20 minutes

Materials/Preparation: Check through the graphic organiser ideas below and think about which of them might be suitable for your students. Practise drawing it on the board.

in class

1. Present to your students the graphic organiser idea that is suitable for your lesson.

Graphic Organisers

A The path
Draw a simple lane or path with a few bends in it like this:

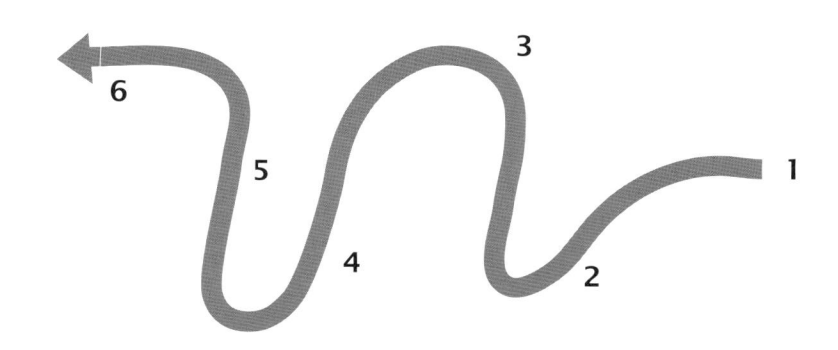

This graphic organiser can help you and students to plan events and essays or to work out a revision time table before an exam. Students can add words, and stick on pictures or post-its, depending on what you use it for.

B The target
Draw some concentric circles. In Rinvolucri and Frank (1990), students write the names of their closest, good and more distant friends in the inner, middle and outside circles of these sociograms and then talk about them. Targets can be used to store other information such as vocabulary of different registers, e.g.:
- inner circle – language for use with close friends
- middle circle – language that is neutral and useful in most situations,
- outer circle – language for use with strangers and those above us in a hierarchy

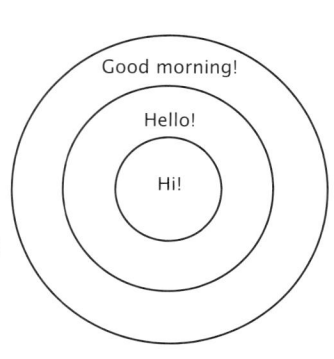

5.11 Graphic organiser variety

C Stars and pie charts
Stars with numbered points and circles divided up like pies can be used for all sorts of things, e.g:
- Self-introduction
  Each number stands for a category of personal information such as:
    - inherited physical characteristic
    - inherited character trait
    - membership of a group
    - what fires me up
    - memories
    - things I tend to notice.

Students then introduce themselves to their partners by talking about one or more points on the star or one or more pieces of their pie.

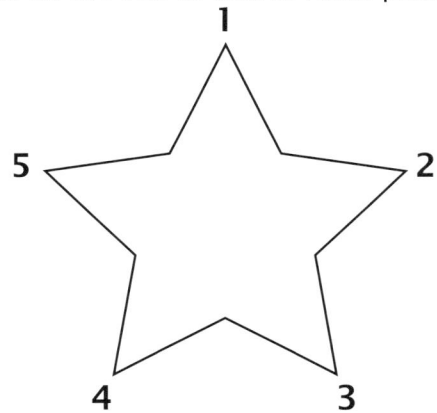

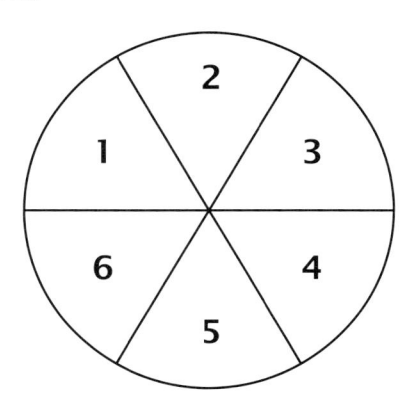

- Story writing
  If students write different question words at the end of each star point (e.g. *what, when, why, who, how, where*), they can then brainstorm crazy answers to each question. Next, they challenge themselves to write a story containing all the elements they came up with in their brainstorm.

- Self-assessment
  A pie can be sliced up into components of a topic. Numbers can be added into each slice and a student can then rate themselves on each component of a piece of work. Thus an English composition could be sliced up into ideas, layout, spelling, grammar, lexical variation, start, middle and end. Students can then rate themselves, after they have written a composition, according to how well they think they have done in each slice, e.g. 5 (top mark) for ideas, but 2 for grammar.

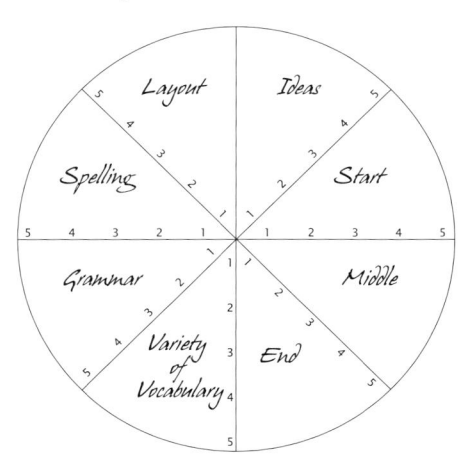

CHAPTER 5: CREATIVE THINKING   169

5.11 Graphic organiser variety

- Review game
  This time, each number stands for a category of recent class work such as grammar, vocabulary, stories, punctuation, pronunciation, discourse. You need to prepare a few questions on each topic. In teams, students choose categories and then try to answer a question from you in that category.

D Vocabulary scales

Take a narrow semantic area such as 'words describing the cost of things in shops'. Draw a scale and elicit the antonyms *cheap* and *expensive* from students. Write them on the scale thus:

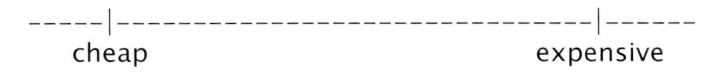

```
-----|-------------------------------|------
cheap                            expensive
```

Explain that the words *cheap* and *expensive* fit into a sentence starting *It's …* or *It was …*

Ask students if they know any other related adjectives or expressions. If they come up with good suggestions, such as *dear* or *reasonable*, add them onto the scale in the right places, thus:

```
-----|---------|---------------|---------|------
cheap   reasonable        dear      expensive
```

If they come up with words that are more appropriate on a different scale (such as *scruffy* which belongs more on the 'tidy-untidy' scale), point this out.

In the scale above, the 'cheap' end looks a bit sparse. Students can now see where their vocabulary is rich and where poor. Over the next few weeks, they can use texts, tapes, you or each other to find more words to fit on the scale (e.g. *a bargain*, *a rip-off* etc). By plotting them onto the scale, they see both the individual and relative meanings of the words and phrases.

Many other semantic areas lend themselves to storage on scales, e.g. words describing the amount of taste in food (tasteless---tasty), moisture in the air (wet---dry), friendliness of people. Ask students to choose areas they are interested in, to keep a Vocabulary Scales notebook and to keep track of their improvement as they learn more and more words for more and more scales.

Once students are used to this way of looking at vocabulary meaning and storage, i.e. working with two poles, mediating categories and working with topics involving perception of the material world, you can move into the non-material world. Introduce scales for, e.g., Human to Animal, Nature to Culture and Life to Death, and enjoy the discussion of the yetis, Peter Rabbits and ghosts that come up as you look for words in the middle of these scales.

Finally, as a little thinking task for you, consider the options below. What could you use the following for in your own work?

5.11 Graphic organiser variety

E A flow chart

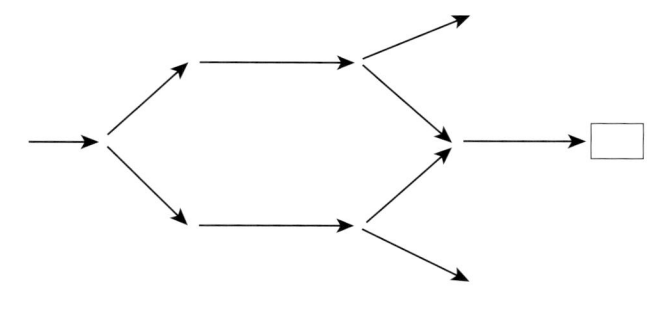

Hint ... to work out some sort of process, procedure or operation?

F A triangle

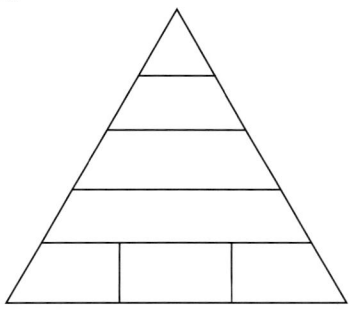

Hint ... to work out some sort of ranking, hierarchy or set of ratios?

G Steps up or down

Hint ... to show a cumulative syllabus or stages in testing?

Note
In this section we have looked at the creation of visuals as one way of supporting our thinking processes. We have also capitalised on mental images by using them for language development. If you are interested in using art to stimulate and thought and self-expression, look at *English Through Art* in this series by Grundy et al (2011).

Acknowledgement
Thanks to Kieran Egan for the non-material use of Graphic Organiser D.

5.12 Inventing new buttons

> Using generative frameworks

Focus: Vocabulary of shapes and materials. Adjective word order. Learning how to use a creativity tool.

Level: Pre-Intermediate upwards

Time: 20 minutes

Materials/Preparation: You need to make sure you have ten ideas for each axis on the diagram in steps 1 to 3.

in class

1. Explain to the class that you are going to help them to become inventors. Then draw a 10 × 10 grid on the board, leaving enough room for ideas to be written along the top of the grid and down the side. Give the grid a title such as *Buttons*.

2. Elicit shapes from the class, e.g. *round*, *square*, *banana-shaped* etc, and draw these along the top of the grid.

3. Elicit materials from the group, e.g. *metal*, *wood*, *chocolate*, *glass*, and write these down the side of the grid.

	○	□	△	☽	☆	▭	⌭			
Metal										
Wood										
Chocolate										
Glass										

CHAPTER 5: CREATIVE THINKING

5.12 Inventing new buttons

4. By reading across and down, 'going along the corridor and up or down the stairs', each cell in the grid now contains a novel button idea, e.g. *a square metal button*, depending on what ideas have been elicited from the class. Ask students to read out a really normal button, or one that they have at home, or one they would like to have, or to invent the strangest, the funniest, or the least practical button they can, using the graph.

5. This may lead students to think of other buttons with attributes different from those on the grid axes. Add extra columns to deal with these genuinely fresh innovations.

Follow-up / Variations

A Instead of inventing new buttons, students can invent, e.g., new ice creams, by substituting *Flavours* and *Add-ons* on the two dimensions of the grid. Thus they can create *carrot ice cream with nuts* or *chocolate ice cream with parsley*.
Simply change the topic and dimensions to suit the interests of your class, whether these be cars, jeans, mobile phones, new offices or whatever. Students can then take the idea on as their own and create many different kinds of things for fun.

B If you write, for example, the names of famous people, or of film, book or cartoon characters across the top and down the side of the grid, students can be asked to find a cell and then either prepare two interesting questions the characters could ask each other or construct a dialogue between them.

Acknowledgements
I learned the main activity from Wragg and Brown (1993, p. 43).
Variation B I learned from Bowker (2007).

5.13 Potato talks

> Using generative frameworks

Focus: Helping students to find things to talk about on a given topic. Speaking and listening.

Level: Pre-Intermediate upwards

Time: 20 minutes

Materials/Preparation: Bring in a potato and an apple, each wrapped separately in a paper bag. Have a mental list of categories of things that could be said about them; see below for ideas.

in class

1. If your students have difficulty thinking of ideas of what to say for talks, oral interviews or conversations, help them by putting a potato where they can see it in front of the class. Write the word *potato* on the board and draw spokes coming from it.

2. Ask students to come up with any sentence they like about the potato. Wait.

3. A student may say, e.g., 'It's brown'. Accept the offering happily and write the word *colour* at the end of one of the spokes. Ask for another sentence. Someone might say 'I don't like them very much!' Write *personal opinion* at the end of a spoke.

4. Continue in this way, hinting at things that could be said about the potato or asking direct questions, e.g. 'How can we cook them?' or 'Does anybody know where they came from originally?' or 'In primary school did you use them to print things?' Every time you have an offering from a student accept it enthusiastically and write down the *class* of contribution at the end of a spoke, e.g. *products*,

5.13 Potato talks

geography, art and craft, types, contents, health etc. Keep going until you have ten or so categories including *history, science, shape, what it's made of, price, politics, different names for* (e.g. *spuds*), *connected expressions in English* (e.g. *couch potato*). Complete this category list yourself if your students don't come up with them all.

5. Next, put students in pairs and ask them to talk about potatoes for three minutes. If they get stuck, they can look at the board and find another category. They should make sure they say something for each category.

6. Once the time is up, congratulate students for keeping going, and ask if anyone thought of anything different to say. Add any new category of comment to those on the board.

7. Ask them to talk again in pairs. But rub out the word *potato* and open your second paper bag. Bring out the apple and place it where they can see it. Write the word *apple* in the centre of the spokes on the board. Set them off for another three minutes.

8. After the time limit is up, ask them what they said under each category and refine any language you need to. Congratulate them again on keeping going. Add any new categories to the board.

9. Give students two minutes to memorise the ten or more categories of comments that are at the end of the spokes on the board. After two minutes, have them close their eyes and see how many they can remember.

Follow-up / Variations
Next lesson, ask students to call out the categories of comments from the lesson above. As they call out *colour, shape, price, personal opinion* etc, write these up on the board. Then put a completely different topic on the board, e.g. *Africa* or *the 1900s* or *mobile phones* or *Johnny Depp*. Set them off talking about the topic in pairs for three minutes.

Once students have learned the categories and have had a couple of practices, let them choose the topics. Also, ask them to work in pairs, changing roles; one person is now the speaker while the other person listens, and if the speaker gets stuck, jogs the speaker's memory about different categories of topic they can talk about.

5.14 Acrostics

> Using generative frameworks

Focus: Giving students a way in to a discussion and raising ideas. Speaking and listening.

Level: Intermediate upwards

Time: 20 minutes

Materials/Preparation: None.

in class

1. Ask students to give you a word in English that has more than around ten letters. When they give you one, write it down the left-hand side of the board in capitals, e.g.:

```
I
N
T
E
R
N
A
T
I
O
N
A
L
```

2. Ask any of the following questions about any of the letters in the word they have given you:
    'What do you need in a homework task that starts with an I?'
    'What's a problem a homework task can have that starts with an N?'
    'What is a great thing to have in a homework task that starts with a T?'

CHAPTER 5: CREATIVE THINKING

5.14 Acrostics

3. Write whatever answers you get by the letter you nominated. Thus, e.g., *interest* by the letter I, *not enough time to do* it by N, *ten out of ten* by T.

4. Ask students what their homework is like; which of these things do they have too much of or too little of, which is a problem, which is a strength and so on. Allow as much talking time as your students want to explain what they mean and give each other ideas and support etc.

Follow-up
Once students are familiar with this idea, they can use it themselves to raise relevant themes and start a discussion on any issue of use and interest to them.

Variations
Acrostics can be made from students' names. Ask people to write their names in capitals down the left-hand side of the page as above. They then write an adjective about themselves or a true phrase about a current interest, starting with each of the letters of their name. They can then read them out to others in the group.
E.g.:
    T-eacher
    E-nglish is one of my subjects
    S-inging is what I do on Tuesday nights
    S-o many kinds of music I like!
    A-nimals are what I am very fond of!
or
    T-rying to write an activity for my fifth chapter now
    E-nglish is the language it is in
    S-pelling is not great
    S-o I use the spell checker on my PC
    A-t the end I will ask a friend to read it through!

5.15 Two similarities, two differences

> Building empathy

Focus: Comparing and contrasting oneself with others. The language of comparisons. Integrated skills.

Level: Pre-Intermediate upwards

Time: 20 minutes

Materials/Preparation: None.

in class

1. Explain that you will soon ask students to talk to each other in pairs to find two things they have in common and two which are different. Explain that these things cannot be visible. So, they cannot compare hair colour and they can't say, 'We both wear glasses.' Instead, they need to ask and answer questions about things that are invisible, such as food preferences or hobbies. Then put students in pairs to find four things.

2. In plenary again, give some examples about yourself and, say, your sister, in order to exemplify the sort of language students will need for the next stage. Put useful phrases up on the board such as:
   She ... , and I ... too.
   We both ...
   Both of us ... (plus plural verb)
   Neither of us ... (singular or plural verb okay)
   She ... (not)*, and I ...* (not) *either.*

3. Ask students, in the same pairs, to write four true sentences on what they found out, using the phrases on the board.

4. Ask some pairs of students to read out some of their sentences.

Variations

A If your students don't know each other well, after step 1 put students into fours and ask them to introduce not themselves but their partner to the other two people in the foursome, using the information gained in step 1.

B At higher levels, increase the number of facts to be found out, add higher level connectors such as *while we both..., whereas ..., on one hand ... but on the other ...*, and ask students to write a text comparing themselves and their partner for homework.

5.16 I am one among many

> Building empathy

Focus: Students learn about their group and their own place within it. Speaking and listening. Question practice. The language of informal survey reports, e.g. *most of us*, *one of us*.

Level: Intermediate upwards

Time: 20 minutes

Materials/Preparation: You need a couple of starter questions (see below for suggestions).

in class

1. Explain that you are all going to ask questions of the class to find out more about it. Start with a question of your own, such as 'How many of you have a relative who speaks some English?' or 'How many of you have been to an English-speaking country?'. Ask students to hold up their hands if they have. You can put up your own hand too if you want to join in and be part of the group, and if you can answer Yes to the question.

2. Count the hands, and on the board write a sentence that reflects the numbers, such as *Some of us have been to an English-speaking country.*

3. Continue with another question such as, 'Who likes music?' and again count hands and write up a sentence on the board that represent the proportion of people who put their hands up, e.g. *Most of us like music. Only one of us hates it!*

4. Encourage students to ask questions to put to the group about things they want to know. Help them to phrase these if necessary. Students may want to ask, e.g., 'Who knows what we have to do for Biology homework?' or 'Who lives near Xville and comes to school by car?' or 'How many people here have an older brother?'.

5. After each question, count the hands that go up and help students to express what is true for the group. Write these appropriate sentences up on the board. Gradually build a repertoire of phrases, depending on student level, from, e.g., *all of us* through *half of us* to *a few of us* to *none of us*.

6. Ask students to copy down all the sentences in their notebooks.

5.16 I am one among many

Follow-up
In later lessons, more questions can be put by individuals to the group. These can contain useful language recently learned, such as Present Simple, Present Perfect, *tend to*, *don't tend to* and *used to*. All the resulting sentences, creating a group profile, can be stored and added to. This can build a sense of community and group identity, and also reminds individuals of 'where they are' within it.

Acknowledgement
A version of this activity appeared in Woodward (2001).

5.17 Questions to the head

> Building empathy

Focus: Encouraging students to think what it would be like to be another very different human being. Speaking and listening. Asking and answering personal questions.

Level: Intermediate upwards

Time: 30 minutes

Materials/Preparation: You need an A4 portrait of an unknown person who is very different in look, age and life experience from your students. Put the portrait on a piece of card. Cut out a piece of blank paper about the size of the face, and clip it onto the portrait, leaving only the edge of the face and the hair, neck, shoulders and periphery details visible. Think up the sorts of questions that might be asked about the person by people seeing this doctored picture, and for levels up to lower intermediate think up some possible answers and make notes on the back of the picture.

in class

1. Choose a student to help you who is capable of stepping into someone else's shoes.

2. Show the rest of the class the partly masked portrait. Ask them to look carefully at whatever they can see of hair, clothing etc.

3. Ask them to write down ten questions they would like to ask the person when that person visits their classroom soon for an interview. You can write some question words on the board to help them, e.g. *what, who, when, why, which, how many, how long, do, did, are, is, have*, depending on what they know. At higher levels, write some more interesting ones such as *What if ...? Supposing ...?* and *I wonder if ...*

4. Once students are settled writing questions, take your chosen student to a quiet corner and secretly show them the whole picture. Help them (for lower levels, using your notes on the back of the picture) to predict the sorts of questions they will be asked by their classmates and the sorts of answers the person in the picture might give. Leave your volunteer to prepare, and go back to help your writing students.

5. Bring in the volunteer, holding the masked picture in front of their face, introduce them as a mystery guest and sit them in front of the class.

5.17 Questions to the head

6. Students then ask their questions, and the volunteer answers them in the role of the person in the picture. Keeping the portrait held up in front of their face will make the interview more lifelike for the rest of the class and will enable the portrait holder to read any notes on the back of the picture.

7. Thank the mystery guest and let them go back to their seat. Ask the students if they would like to see the whole portrait. If they would, show it to them.

Follow-up
1. Students discuss, in small groups or plenary, what they have learned about the mystery guest.

2. Students write a summary of what they have learned. If the person in the portrait was from a definite cultural group, (e.g. Native North American) or specific population (e.g. a prisoner), students can research that before writing to make their work factually correct.

Variations
A The questions to the head can be written for homework and checked by you before the interview takes place in class. The protagonist can prepare for homework, too, as long as you can trust them not to reveal too much to classmates before the follow-up class. (If they did, it would take away the useful element of surprise and mystery.)

B Students can choose portraits and prepare a role play. They may well choose pictures of celebrities, which will mean some students may know quite a lot about the person in the picture.

C Instead of using a partially covered picture, you can sketch the outline of an androgynous figure on the board. Students brainstorm characteristics, and these are written up inside the figure. Students then brainstorm external factors such as appearance, context or influences, and these are written up around the figure. Continue until a character has been created. Students can then write a short paragraph about the character, or can discuss what kind of house, weekend, job or holiday the character might like.

Acknowledgements
I learned the main activity from John Morgan. A version of this activity appeared in Lindstromberg (2004). I learned variation C from the Department of Education and Skills MFL Learning Unit web site.

5.18 What are they really thinking?

> Building empathy

Focus: Subverting adverts by considering what the people who are models in them are really thinking. Speaking and writing. Vocabulary development.

Level: Intermediate upwards

Time: 20 minutes

Materials/Preparation: You need a collection of magazine picture adverts. For the follow-up, find out about the Bubble Project on the internet. The manifesto and some of the examples on www.thebubbleproject.com are excellent, but there is very rude language in some of the thought bubbles so be careful to check through these first before, e.g., flashing them up by data projector in your classroom!

in class

1. Put the word *advert* on the board, and elicit and teach some useful connected words such as *eye-catching, poster, persuade somebody to buy something, slogan* and *logo*.

2. If you have space, lay out all the adverts on tables and invite students to come and look at them. If not, display just a few adverts centrally where students can see them and look at them together.

3. Elicit or teach any words for key items in the adverts that students don't know.

4. Ask students to look at one of the people in one of the adverts. What are they supposed to be doing, feeling, saying and thinking? For example, students may say that a woman in one advert is wearing a swimsuit, smoothing her legs and smiling; she is supposed to be thinking 'Wow, this sun cream is excellent! My legs are all brown and smooth and silky. I feel terrific!'

5. Ask students to imagine how many hours the swimsuit model has been sitting still, and if they think she is tired or cold or hungry. Does she like the swimsuit she is wearing? Does she like all the stuff on her legs? Then draw a thought bubble on the board, and ask students to imagine what she is really thinking, such as 'I want to go home and have a hot bath' or 'I'm happy I get £500 for today!' or 'This stuff smells terrible!' or 'I wish I had a sweater!' Write up each suggestion in a thought bubble.

5.18 What are they really thinking?

6. Ask students to choose another of the adverts and to write a thought bubble for the person in the picture reflecting what they are perhaps really thinking.

7. Share the thought bubbles among the whole class.

Follow-up
1. Students can bring in other adverts cut out of magazines or newspapers. If they are digitally literate, they can bring in TV adverts, possibly as video clips from the internet. They can do a short presentation on what the advert is for and what the person in it is supposed to be doing, thinking and feeling, and then what they might really be thinking.

2. You can tell students about the Bubble Project.

Variation
If you cut the slogans and brand names off the pictures before class, you can ask students to guess what they think the adverts are for, and try to match each picture with its cut-off slogan before step 4.

Acknowledgement
I first read about Ji Lee's Bubble Project and how to use it in class in Keddie (2008).

5.19 Half a conversation

> Building empathy

Focus: Empathising with others, based on hints contained in normal speech. Practising a dialogue.

Level: Intermediate upwards

Time: 30 minutes

Materials/Preparation: You need a one-sided dialogue such as the one below.

in class

1. Ask students if they are ever in places where they hear someone talking on a mobile phone. Discuss how strange or interesting it is to hear just one side of a conversation. How much can one guess about what the other person is saying?

2. Hand out half a dialogue, such as the one below:

> A:
> B: Yes, it's me!
> A:
> B: I'm on the train.
> A:
> B: I'm coming home.
> A:
> B: About midnight. What time do *you* think it is?
> A
> B: Well, *I* think it's early.
> A:
> B: I was at Jane's place.
> A:
> B: Her party. I told you! Remember?
> A:
> B: That's not fair!
> A:
> B: It's breaking up. We're going into a tunnel. I can't hear you. I'll see you in a bit.
> Hmmmmmmm! (Puts phone away)

CHAPTER 5: CREATIVE THINKING

5.19 Half a conversation

3. Ask students to read B's part silently and then to guess what the conversation is about, who A and B are, what relationship they have to each other and how they might both be feeling. Tell the students they will need to justify their guesses in the next step.

4. Work with the whole class to discuss the situation.

5. Elicit what A may possibly have said at the start of the conversation. Accept any possible ideas, such as 'Is that you?'

6. Work on A's next utterance in the same way. Accept anything like 'Where are you?' or 'Where on earth are you?'

7. Put students, in pairs, to work on guessing A's remarks in the next part of the dialogue in the same way.

8. Discuss their ideas in the whole class. Explain why particular guesses will work or not work by looking ahead to B's next utterance and seeing if it follows well and by considering the mood and relationship between the two people.

9. Once the whole dialogue has been filled in with possible utterances for A's part, check whether the students' answers to the questions in step 3 are still the same or if they have altered slightly. Discuss how A and B might be feeling, and what they might say to each other when B finally gets home.

10. Students can write a possible dialogue for B's return home and role play the scene in pairs. You can add a restriction, if you wish, such as it must have a good outcome!

5.20 Your festival or mine?

> Building empathy

Focus: Learning about festivals in different countries. Considering how people worldwide are similar or different. Integrated skills. Question formation. Present Simple. Vocabulary development.

Level: Pre-Intermediate upwards

Time: 20 minutes each lesson in several lessons

Materials/Preparation: For step 1, find the name of a festival in your students' home country or countries.

For step 2, find a sound or video recording, or a text with pictures, of a festival that is new to you (e.g. the Palio, Siena, Italy; the Tomato Festival, Spain; Children's Day, Japan; Diwali, India; Fasnacht, Switzerland; the Water Festival, Thailand; the Monkey Festival, Thailand; Chinese New Year, many countries; the Day of the Dead, Mexico; or May Day, England). You need to familiarise yourself with the festival for step 3.

For variation A, prepare a set of cards with information on them about different sorts of people, e.g. an energetic university student who loves adventure, a mother with a young child, a pair of newly-weds with very little money, a recently retired teacher.

Students will need access to the internet for their homework research.

in class

1. Ask students if they know the word *festival* and if they know of any examples. If they don't, help them with this, naming an example of a festival in their country.

2. Explain that you are going to answer questions about a festival that you have only just found out about yourself and which is in a country that's unfamiliar to your students. What questions could they ask you about it? Every time a student comes up with a good question such as *What's it called?* or *Where is it?* or *How long does it last?* write it on the board and ask students to copy it down. Explain that they too will be learning about a new festival soon and will be answering the same questions from their classmates.

3. Students then ask you questions about 'your' festival. Answer the questions as best you can. If you don't know the answer to some, promise to find out.

5.20 Your festival or mine?

4. Show your videos or pictures, or play your recording. Finally, let students read any text you have on the festival. Discuss what they have learned about it. Teach or review any useful vocabulary that has come up.

5. Elicit other questions students could ask about festivals in future, e.g.:

> - How do people prepare for the festival?
> - Do people eat special food or wear special clothes?
> - Is there any music?
> - What happens?
> - Is it dangerous in any way?
> - What is the high point?
> - How long has the festival existed?
> - What does it mean?
> - What is it for?
> - Who is it for?
> - How many people go?
> - Are there any special objects or animals involved?

These questions can form a handout useful for note-taking in later lessons (see follow-up step 2).

6. Put the names of some more festivals on the board. Ask who would like to find out about which one, or assign them. Students can work alone or in pairs. For homework, they should find out as much as possible about one festival and prepare to tell the class about it. They can write a short text to hand in for correction before their presentation to aid confidence, if they prefer. Set a time limit for the presentations.

Follow-up

1. Take in any texts and make sure the first presenters are well prepared before scheduling part of a class for this. It is a good idea to pre-screen any videos they would like to show in class, just to make sure they are not too long or in any way unsuitable to show students.

2. Keep aside a part of a lesson for the first presentation. First of all, review your own festival and provide the extra information that you did not have last time. Then introduce the presenter(s) of the next festival. Let the class ask them questions from their handout and make notes on it. Keep any videos until last; knowing they're on the way will keep motivation high. Finally, set a date for the next presenter(s).

5.20 Your festival or mine?

3. Different students can present different festivals over a period of weeks.

4. Once quite a few festivals have been introduced, ask students what things tend to be the same about most festivals (people have time off work, they do something completely different from normal, they eat special food), which things often differ, (objects have different symbolic significance, ingredients will be local), which festival they personally would like to go to / would not like to go and why, and which festival they think other people they know would like to go to / not go to and why.

Variations

A Once students have learned about several festivals, hand out your people cards. The students should consider which of the festivals learnt about so far they would recommend these people to go to.

B Ask students to dream up a brand new festival for their best friend. They need to choose a date and a name for it. Then they should figure out how long it would last, where it might be held and what could happen. For homework they design a poster advertising their new festival.

Acknowledgement
I got the idea for variation A from Mei Lin.

CHAPTER 6
THINKING CLEARLY ABOUT TEXTS AND SITUATIONS

Students are positively swimming in emails, texts, phone messages, flyers, newspapers and magazines these days. Some actively enjoy this plethora. Others can at times find the volume and ubiquity of these communications unsettling. The information contained in them may also be inaccurate or misleading, and may even be designed on occasion to manipulate us. So students need to check the provenance and credibility of these messages, spot their good points, biases, assumptions and implications, and consider alternatives before using them to increase their knowledge base or enjoyment. Otherwise they may feel overloaded, be persuaded of something against their better judgement or even fall prey to scams.

It is thus a useful skill for them to learn to think clearly about texts in our EFL classes. Other types of texts that we use in class, such as poems, plays, short stories and graded readers, may be a bit of a challenge to our learners, so we can help them to get the maximum amount out of these as well. It's good, too, for us all to be aware of our own background assumptions and to see how these colour our reception of information, ideas and opinions.

In this chapter we will consider practical activities to help with some basic questions such as:
- Where does a text come from?
- Is it balanced or biased?
- Does it contain fact or opinion?
- Is it accurate?
- Am *I* balanced or biased?
- How can I build knowledge?
- What is the right thing to do?
- How can I interpret proverbs, quotations and stories? and
- How can I think clearly about challenging situations?

Teaching Tips

TT1 **Stories**

Stories free us from the here and now, but are also lifelike. They can be a powerful and many-layered means for us to understand the world, ourselves and others. When choosing stories, find ones that:
- are clear,
- are funny or interesting,
- are well-structured,
- have a good story line,
- have believable and sympathetic characters, and
- have vivid language within the grasp of your students.

Possible sources are: Aesop's fables (e.g. 'The Crow and the Pitcher', 'The Dog in the Manger'), Nasreddin Hodja stories, traditional folk and fairy stories, children's stories, poems, collections of pictures and objects, TV soaps and songs. See also Fisher, 1996 and 1999, and Morgan and Rinvolucri, 1983.

It's a good idea to store stories in skeleton form so that each time you use one or tell one it comes out fresh. You will want to make a note of any language you particularly wish to use. Here is an example of a stored story skeleton:

The bucket
Teacher wants to make special point to students
T asks for big bucket. Students bring it.
T asks for rocks. Students bring them.
Lots of rocks in bucket.
T asks 'Is it full?'
Students say yes/no.
T asks for sand & pours it in
T asks, 'Is it full?'
Asks for water, pours it in.
Is it full?
Nobody can think of anything else to go in bucket.
T asks, 'Why did I ask you to do all this? What's the point?'

Ask students this ... WAIT for their answers!
Possible answers? ...
- If you don't put the big things in first you will never get them in. (priorities)
- No matter how busy you are you can always fit one more interesting thing in! (challenge self)
- No matter how full you are after dinner you can always squeeze in dessert!

Teaching Tips

We can all have the same experience (story), but we have different thoughts about it.

To see how you can get the best from stories in the language learning classroom, try activity 6.11.

6.1 Where does it come from?

> Origins

Focus: Encouraging students to find out the provenance of texts. Text-related vocabulary and question development.

Level: Pre-Intermediate upwards

Time: 20 minutes

Materials/Preparation: A worksheet based perhaps on the one below, but adapted for your students' level and for the material you are analysing.

in class

1. Before the class launches into a book that you plan to use a lot, such as a course book or graded reader, encourage students to handle it and to turn it over to see where different information about it is to be found, e.g. help them to find the back-cover blurb, the publishing details and the author information. Help them at this point with key vocabulary such as *cover*, *publisher*, *chapter*, *subheading*.

2. Give them a worksheet such as the one below, and ask them to answer the questions on it.

Finding out about a book
- Who wrote the book?
- What can you find out about the author, e.g. country, first language, age, experience, qualifications?
- Why did the writer write this book?
- What interest does the author have in the topic?
- Who published the book, where and when?
- Do your answers to the questions so far make a difference to how you feel about the information, ideas and opinions in the book?
- Who and what does the introduction say the book is for?
- What are the main text divisions?
- Is there a good contents page/system of subheadings/index so that you can find things easily?

Read the first line/paragraph/chapter or the introduction and the last line/paragraph/chapter or the conclusion.
- What can this book help you with?
- What can this book NOT help you with?
- Does the author recommend other sources of information?
- What questions would you like, or do you need, to ask to learn from this book?

6.1 Where does it come from?

3. Go through the answers with students, discussing issues such as whether new books are necessarily better than old ones, whether books written in one part of the world are right for people in another, whether financial interests are important to content etc.

4. Ask students when they think this kind of checking might be useful to them in other lessons or outside class.

5. Move on to work with the material in your normal way.

Follow-ups
Once students have gone through the worksheet with one book, they can be asked to make a bibliographical entry modelled on ones acceptable in your context, for homework.

They can also use the worksheet with other books, perhaps ones they use in other school subjects.

Variations
This activity can be used, with an adapted worksheet, to help students discover more about the provenance of comics, magazines, graded readers, websites such as Wikipedia, radio and TV programmes, and national and regional newspapers.

6.2 Balancing the books

> Balance

Focus: Raising students' awareness of the balance – or lack of it – in materials. Vocabulary connected to the chosen topic (see below). Scanning texts. Speaking and listening.

Level: Intermediate upwards

Time: 30 minutes

Materials/Preparation: Gather the materials you would like students to analyse, e.g. their own course book, a newspaper, a set of articles on a single topic, tourist information about their own area or a number of magazine adverts. Decide on the focus for analysis (see step 2).

in class

1. Put students into groups of three and give them the material that you would like them to analyse.

2. Ask students to count something in the material, their choice depending on the chosen focus; it could be the presence of people of different nationalities, cultural stereotypes, mentions of or allusions to health or unemployment, or anything that is useful for your students to think about. For example, if you are interested in raising their awareness of gender imbalance in learning materials, ask them to take their course book and check:
   - the number of women and men authors
   - how many images of women and men are in the text
   - the types of activity woman and men are engaged in throughout the stories, situations and pictures
   - how many times the words *she*, *he*, *woman*, *man*, *girl*, *boy* are mentioned
   - the number of times women and men speak, who starts the turn and how long it is
   - the number of turns in conversations
   - the number of times women or men interrupt each other.

   Ask students to keep a note of the numbers counted.

3. Once students have done this, ask them what they have found out and see if there have been any surprises. Explain that counting is considered fairly objective, since it's likely that different people counting the same things in the same materials will come up with roughly similar numbers. The drawbacks to counting are that it teaches us nothing about context or the reasons why imbalances occur.

6.2 Balancing the books

4. Next, ask students to code the material. Coding is when you define a category and then go through materials looking for it. Here are some categories students could define and look for on the topic of gender:
   - active versus passive characters
   - major versus minor characters
   - stereotyped versus unstereotyped images
   - high- or low-status activities.

5. Once they have done some coding, bring the class back together. Again, see if there are any surprises. Explain that because personal definitions are involved, coding raises more questions about objectivity than counting does.

6. Finally work with students to 'qualitatively analyse' the material. This means they try, with your help, to arrive at a more complete picture of who a piece of material seems to be aimed at and why. Encourage them to look at:
   - juxtapositions of image and text
   - plot types
   - characters and how they are depicted, what they say and do
   - vocabulary and topic choice.

7. Again, see what they have found and what they think. Be good-humoured and non-judgemental about whatever students raise, or you may put some students off doing this kind of work again.

Follow-up
Now that they have the idea, students can choose the sets of material they want to analyse (such as blurbs on the back of CDs by their favourite bands and web sites connected to their own school), and the issue(s) they want to focus on (e.g. portrayal of young people, or representation of their favourite sport or hobby). A short project can be set to encourage them to work on this.

Notes
Qualitative analysis is both very subjective and very revealing. It's the sort of work that activists in any minority or marginalised social group can do in a flash and which those in the majority or dominant social groups take a long time to understand.

I remember sitting in a cinema some years ago watching a film with some black colleagues. 'Ah look!' I said, 'There's a black character!' I was pleased; things were getting better in the world, I thought. But my colleagues were looking at their watches and making bets that the black character would be dead inside ten minutes. He was. (See Woodward, 2003.)

6.3 Fact or opinion?

> The truth of the matter

Focus: Helping students to think about and express thoughts on the differences between fact and opinion. Language associated with the topic (see below).

Level: Pre-Intermediate upwards

Time: 30 minutes

Materials/Preparation: Think up a few sentences about your classroom. Some of the sentences should be demonstrably true, such as *There are two windows* if indeed there are. Some sentences should be a matter of opinion, for example *This is a nice room*. You will also need some copies of a picture of a room with some furniture and some personal objects in it and some statements of fact and of opinion connected to the picture (see examples in step 3).

in class

1. Ask students to listen to a few things that you say about the classroom, or any other single subject, (or write these up on the board and ask your students to read them). The two types of sentence should be mixed as you present them to the class. Ask students to think how they would divide the sentences up into two different groups.

2. Elicit from students what they think the two different groups are, and why. If students suggest different groupings, such as one group of sentences being about colours and another group being about size, accept the ideas gracefully but keep going until you are offered a division between facts (or *things that are true* or *things which you can see* or however your students explain this) and those that are opinion (or *what you think but I don't think* or however your students explain this).

3. Divide students into groups of three or four. Give each group the picture of the room.

CHAPTER 6: THINKING CLEARLY ABOUT TEXTS AND SITUATIONS

6.3 Fact or opinion?

Also give them your list of sentences about the picture, some of which are facts and some of which are opinions. The sentences can contain target language that you wish students to use later on, such as:
- It is (large / small / cosy / clean).
- This room belongs to a (singer / woman / person who loves …).
- It's quite / very / rather (nice / stuffy / light).
- It's got (a window / a door / lots of desks).
- On the (walls / floor) / In the (middle / corner) there is / are …
- The (walls / ceiling / bed / chair) are / is …
- This person has / likes / wears (glasses, blue, casual clothes).

Students are to divide the sentences into two groups, fact or opinion, and also to guess what sort of person the room belongs to.

4. In plenary, ask students for their thoughts. Write up useful language for the reasoning stage either just before or as students work on this. E.g.
   - I think it is a fact because you can see / measure / check / hear / touch /…
   - I think it's an opinion because you think this but I don't … and you can't see it or measure it.
   - I think the person living here is a singer because …

5. Ask students when in real life they think this skill of telling fact from opinion might be useful. They may suggest things like history lessons, when listening to the 'information' in adverts or on the news, and discussions with friends.

Follow-up
For homework, using sentence starters from step 3, students can write about a picture that they choose, cut out or draw themselves. They can challenge other students or the teacher to guess what sort of person the room belongs to.

Variations

A In step 1 above you could choose a different topic, e.g. *people*, and, starting with yourself, provide factual sentences such as *I am wearing a blue top*, if indeed you are. For the opinion sentences you can offer ones like *I am incredibly beautiful / handsome!* In step 3 you would then provide a picture of a person with accompanying fact and opinion sentences. Students could guess what sort of job the person does or what their favourite hobby is.

B Instead of using pictures and teacher-made sentences for students to divide up, you can give students a text and ask them to mark the statements of fact within it in one way and the statements of opinion in another. A good example text is this one, adapted from Sayed, 2010.

6.3 Fact or opinion?

> The reasons for my success in table tennis were speed, mental strength and reflexes. It was a triumph of individuality. This of course is the way people at the top of sports choose to tell their stories. We live in a culture that encourages this sort of thinking. But if I retell my story with the things I didn't mention the first time, I have to say that the table, my brother, my teacher and my club were the important factors. It is the opportunity and the practice not the genes or natural talent that brings success.

This sort of text is harder to mark up and leads to lots of discussion.

C Ask students to copy out phrases from a text into a table under columns marked *Fact* and *Opinion*. Then ask them:
- How could the facts be verified?
- How could the opinions be supported?
- What would it take for them to agree to an opinion? – more people, such as relatives, friends or famous people, who agreed?

D Proverbs such as *A stitch in time saves nine* can be discussed to see whether they represent fact or opinion. (See also activity 6.9 for more work with proverbs.)

E At higher levels, phrases from a text or interview can be noted down and their function also noted, e.g.:

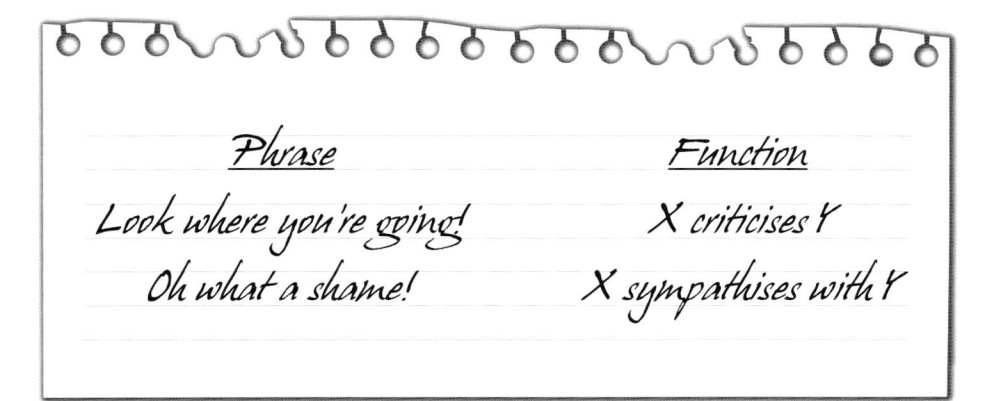

Phrase	Function
Look where you're going!	X criticises Y
Oh what a shame!	X sympathises with Y

Acknowledgements
I learned the main activity from Lin and Mackay, 2004. I learned variations B, C and D from Paran, 2003.

6.4 Spot the smuggled mistake!

> Deception

Focus: Reading. Encouraging students to question the veracity of information. Question formation.

Level: Pre-Intermediate upwards

Time: 20 minutes plus homework and follow-up

Materials/Preparation: Some short texts that contain errors of fact or debatable points. Internet access, or a range of reference books such as dictionaries and encyclopedias (for steps 4 and 6).

in class

1. Write up a sentence on the board such as:
   Elmstead Castle was built by Edward V in 1312.
   Ask students to copy it down. The chances are that they will do this without too much thought or questioning.

2. Ask students to discuss, in pairs, what facts in the sentence could be wrong. Ask them to form questions about those parts of the text.

3. Ask students to call out possible areas of inaccuracy using their questions, e.g.:
   - Is there a place called Elmstead?
   - Is there a castle at Elmstead?
   - Was there an Edward V?
   - Did he reign in 1312?
   - Is it possible for one person to build a castle all by himself?

4. Ask students how they could check the answers to their questions. (If you have internet access and a data projector in your room, you could quickly check online. Otherwise use encyclopaedias, dictionaries and knowledgeable people.) Discuss what is discovered and any surprises. Congratulate students on spotting your attempts to 'smuggle' wrong facts into the work.

5. Give the students a fresh text containing one or more factual errors or debatable points. Remind them of the main question words in English – *what, who, when, where, how, which, why* – in case these prompt further thoughts. Again in pairs, students consider all the things that could be wrong in the text and make notes on these.

6.4 Spot the smuggled mistake!

6. Elicit some possible probing questions from students. At lower levels, give them some specific web sites or short texts to read so that they can check if the information in the text is true. Again, congratulate them on spotting any smuggled errors. At higher levels students can do their own research for homework.

7. Ask students when in real life they think this skill of questioning facts or spotting errors in facts might be useful. They may suggest things like before signing a contract, in political debates, when listening to the 'information' in adverts or on the news, and in discussions with friends.

Follow-ups
1. If students did the research for homework, in a follow-up lesson discuss what they found out.

2. Students can then, in class or for homework, do some research and write short texts themselves which contain one or more factual errors. They should write the texts so that it is hard to spot the errors; in other words, the texts should sound plausible. In a further follow-up lesson, students read out their texts to classmates, who get points for the number of factual errors they spot being smuggled into the texts. You could also give points to those who can correct the factual errors.

Variations
A This idea can be used with texts containing pseudo-scientific statements, e.g. *Drinking increases your chances of dying.* Students can be encouraged to pick holes in texts of this sort by asking questions such as 'Drinking *what* increases our chances of dying? – water? What chances have we all got of dying with or without drinking? If we don't drink anything at all, what will happen?'

Here are some short texts for further practice:
- Buy one bar of chocolate for 64p but pay £1.95 and get THREE bars!
- All Past Simple verbs in English end with *-ed*.
- The correct spelling is *acomadation*.
- I've got a headache.
- Learners only have to turn up in class to be good students.
- Teachers know everything.
- Five helpings of fruit and vegetables a day are essential for health.
- Water boils when you heat it.

6.4 Spot the smuggled mistake!

B Instead of spotting mistakes, students can be encouraged to spot assumptions. So in the question *Do you want milk or juice?* the assumptions are that you are thirsty and that you must choose between those two alternatives. In the following example sentences there are strong background assumptions, too: *Unlike her sister, Dotty is musical* and *He's from Kenya, so he's bound to be good at long-distance running.*

Acknowledgements
I learned the main idea from Paran, 2003. Variation A I learned from Jim Carmichael.

6.5 Which text is right?

> Different perspectives

Focus: Learning about point of view, fact and opinion. Reading and speaking.

Level: Pre-Intermediate upwards

Time: 30 minutes

Materials/Preparation: You need two different texts on the same topic, for example two very different reviews of the same film (see steps 2 and 4 below).

in class

1. Using sound, visual or word prompts, introduce the topic of your texts and ask students what they know about it.

2. Give out the first text and ask students to read it. Here is an example text about an animation film:

   > *Avatar* cost a lot of money to make. It is very long. Technically brilliant, it tries to do too much. The characters are weak. The story is copied from *Dances with Wolves*. Don't bother!

3. Make sure in your usual ways that students understand the text. Then ask them if they would like to see the film reviewed, or if they have already seen it whether or not they agree with the opinion expressed in the text.

4. Repeat steps 2 and 3 with the second, very different, text on the same topic. Here is an example text:

   > *Avatar* ... WOW! Go and see it! Then go and see it again! Beautiful pictures. Something for everyone in your family! What entertainment!

6.5 Which text is right?

5. Once students have read and commented on both texts, ask them a number of questions, such as:
   - What is the same about the two texts and what is different?
   - What cold, hard facts are there in the texts?' (e.g. is there any information on how much the tickets cost, exactly how long the film is, who is in it, where it is set, what the plot is? The answer is 'No', by the way!)
   - So, which text is right?

Finally ask where in life they might see other examples of different texts on the same subjects.

Follow-up
1. For homework, students can find or write two different texts about another film, and then discuss in class the amount of accurate fact and substantiated or unsubstantiated opinion in them.

2. Students can do some research and then write a balanced text of their own with accurate facts and substantiated opinions in it.

Variations
The two or more different texts used can be about graded readers, CDs, video games, items in the news, bands, concerts, products or anything else that interests or is useful to your students.

Notes
The internet is a wonderful source of news and reviews which you can read yourself and then simplify for students if necessary. Just type in the name of the topic you are interested in and take your pick. The web site www.amazon.co.uk has sets of the most helpful, favourable and critical reviews for many titles, thus giving natural material for pro and con texts.

6.6 Through my eyes *or* Am I biased?

> Personal perspectives

Focus: Encouraging students to consider the difference that one's background can make to the way one sees things. Vocabulary development and discussion language.

Level: Intermediate upwards

Time: 30 minutes

Materials/Preparation: Think of a topic that will interest students. You also need to prepare related vocabulary and questions (see step 5 for suggestions).

in class

1. Show some pictures of the sorts of places that people tend to emigrate to from the country where you are based. Check if you have any students in class whose parents or grandparents have emigrated from one country to another. If you have, tell them you will ask them about that later on.

2. Ask students individually to consider generally why people emigrate to other countries. Ask them to make a list of what these people might expect to find in the new country they go to.

3. In pairs, students compare lists and justify the items on them.

4. Ask students about what is on their lists and why they have written these items. Write up some of the most common ideas on the board. Ideas may include *better weather*, *more jobs*, *gaining a better standard of living*.

5. Take one of these topics and write up some questions connected to it, e.g.:
    - What do *you* mean by a 'better standard of living'?
    - Why would this be important to the migrant?
    - Why are workers in some countries paid more than in others?
    - Do you think the people in the countries people go to have the same understanding of a 'better standard of living' as the migrants?

    Ask the whole class what they think about these questions. Bring out the fact that though most people in the world want the same sorts of things, such as health, work, shelter and peace, definitions and views on these same issues can be very different depending on where you come from. Texts written from different places will thus assume very different perspectives.

6.6 Through my eyes or Am I biased?

6. Repeat this sort of discussion with another of the list items such as *better weather* or *more jobs*.

7. Mention that when reading texts by writers from different places it is a good idea to remember how differently we see texts.

Follow-up
Students can be asked to write a short text on what they think about the topic and why where they come from plays a part in what they think.

Meet the students whose parents or grandparents have emigrated from one country to another. Ask them if they would like to write a short text, just for you, on which ways they feel they are part of the country they are in and in which ways they are part of the country their parents and grandparents came from, too.

Variations
You can use the same basic procedure above with any topic that has global implications, e.g. *clean water*, *money rich time poor*, *running out of resources*, *global warming*, *genetic modification*, *endangered species* or *a good diet*.

Acknowledgement
I learned this from Lima, 2009.

6.7 General knowledge building

> Finding out

Focus: Using research, reading and discussion to build general knowledge. Question formation and language development connected to the topic (see below).

Level: Intermediate upwards

Time: 15 minutes in each of a number of lessons, plus homework

Materials/Preparation: You need a topic that neither you nor the students know very much about, a few starter questions, and a short text or a web site about it (see step 4 for a suggestion).

in class

Lesson One

1. Write the topic up on the board and ask if anybody knows anything about it. (An example could be *Guerrilla Gardening*.) If anyone does know about it, ask them to tell the others.

2. If nobody knows, ask if anybody can guess what it is. Wait. See what students come up with.

3. Encourage students to look at each word and to call out words they associate with each one; write these up near the appropriate word on the board. So, for example, students might call out 'war', 'fighting' or 'soldiers'. Write these up near the word *guerrilla*. Students might call out 'What my mum does outside our house' or 'What the men do in the city park'. Write these up near the word *gardening* and ask the students what they now think guerrilla gardening is. Accept all offerings gracefully.

4. Next, either give out a short text on guerrilla gardening (see below) or, alternatively, say a few words about it yourself.

> **Guerrilla gardening**
> Thousands of people all over the world leave their own homes and go to land that they do not own. The land may be big or small. When they get there, they work that land. They clean it up and plant seeds. They grow things there on land that does not belong to them. Sometimes they take what they produce. Sometimes they don't.

6.7 General knowledge building

5. Ask students to come up with as many questions as possible about the topic. You can prompt this by writing up question words on the board such as: *who, what, why, when, where, which, how, what if, supposing, is, are, did, do*. E.g. *Who does this? Why do they do it? What do they grow?* Students write the questions down in a special part of their notebooks. Tell students that your joint aim – since you too do not know the answer to many of the questions – is to find out the answers to the questions together over the next few days / weeks / months.

6. Ask students to search, for homework, amongst their relatives' books at home or on the internet to find out the answers to some of the questions. Alternatively, give them another, longer text to read.

Follow-ups
1. In follow-up lessons, ask students what they have found out, tell them what you have found out, and bring in any pictures, texts and examples that you find for them to read in class or for homework. In short, gradually build knowledge together of the subject. Enjoy the novelty and the surprises. Teach whatever language is needed as you go along and as it arises.

2. You can use this work and apply what they have learned in activity 6.3 to help students to discriminate between fact and opinion, in activity 6.5 to work with texts expressing different opinions on the same topic, in activity 6.4 to help them spot mistakes and assumptions, and in activity 6.8 to discuss the moral issues connected to the topic.
   When you get to discussion, you may also want to look back at chapter 3 TT4 and activities 3.1–3.3 to remind yourself of exploratory talk, and activity 2.4 for concept-stretching ideas.

3. After some time on the topic, students can write a text on what they have learned about it.

4. Once you and the class have dealt with two or three topics, you can consolidate the work done in the ways below:
   - You and the students make up questions on the topics. Keep the questions for a few weeks and then run a general knowledge quiz based on them.
   - Give students a pile of slips of paper, each with information about one of the different topics. Ask them to put the slips in the envelope which is labelled with the correct topic. Thus, slips containing information on guerrilla gardening should go in the envelope marked *Guerrilla Gardening*.

6.7 General knowledge building

- Ask students to come to the front of the class and take a question, written on a slip of paper, from an envelope labelled with whichever topic they feel most confident about. They then try to answer the question. Classmates judge if they are right.

If you knew very little about the topic yourself when you started, then include yourself in these review activities!

Variations

A Other topics might be *the Slow City movement, the No Logo movement, Dieter Rams' ten principles of good design, free diving, free running, cloud appreciation, Freecycle* and *street pastors*.

B Rather than finding out as much as possible about a relatively new development, you can take a modern-day commonplace such as (dental) anaesthesia. Encourage students to trace the idea of pain relief back into the past, through laughing gas and chloroform to alcohol and stoicism. Once you have gone backwards as far as you can, encourage students to think forwards to consider what developments might come next, e.g. patient administered pastes or slow-release patches. The key questions here are:
  - What do we have now?
  - What do we know about it?
  - What came before it?
  - And before that?
  - What could come next?

Other good topics for this *continuations* theme are: *bikes, prisons, pills, toys or games* and *credit cards*.

Note
Verbal skill is known to be a chief constituent of adult success and effectiveness. But verbal skill is not ... simply a how-to skill. It is largely a knowledge-based skill. (Hirsch, 2010)

Acknowledgement
For more on guerrilla gardening see Reynolds, 2008.

6.8 What's the right thing to do?

> Making decisions

Focus: Discussion based on a moral dilemma. Use of opinions language plus *should / ought to*. Vocabulary development related to the topic.

Level: Upper Intermediate

Time: 20 minutes

Materials/Preparation: You need a text containing a moral dilemma (see step 4 for an example).

in class

1. Write the word *Ethics* on the board and ask students what they know about it.

2. Write up any connected ideas that come up. Alternatively, write some up yourself. These might include *Difference between good and bad, right/wrong/evil*, *Being good/honest/decent/moral*, *Having a strong character*, *Being fair*.

3. Explain that you are going to ask the class later to consider a situation where different sorts of behaviour are possible. Recall with the group the sort of language that can be used to express an opinion about an action and then justify it. E.g. 'I think X should … because …'

4. Read or give out a text containing a situation or scenario such as the one below.

> *A busy, well-off man living in the suburbs sometimes asks local people to help him with house and garden tasks like mowing the lawn, weeding the flower beds, washing the car, shopping, cleaning etc. In the summer holidays, he gets young teenagers to help him. In school term-time he asks single mothers, retired people, unemployed people, in fact, anyone who needs the money, to help him. It depends who is available when he needs the help.*
> *He pays the adults £8 per hour. He pays the teenagers £4 per hour. A neighbour was chatting to him one day and found out about this. The neighbour told the man he thought it was wrong; the neighbour thought that anybody who does a job should get paid the same no matter who or how old they are.*
> *What do you think?*

6.8 What's the right thing to do?

5. Make sure in your usual ways that the students understand the situation and the moral dilemma involved. Then put them into small groups and ask them to discuss how much they think the man should pay different people and why. They should not stop at just one idea or opinion but should try to think of as many as possible.

6. Ask each group to give their opinions and reasons. As they do this, one by one, write up their ideas on the board, refining the language as you go if necessary. So if a student says. 'Adults get more money because they know good plant and bad plant for garden', you could write up *Adults should get paid more because they know more about gardening, e.g. they can tell plants from weeds.*

7. Once all the ideas are up, count them and congratulate the students on finding so many. Tell them you are going to write down the number of ideas so that next time they have a similar discussion on a different topic they can aim for even more ideas. Then make a note of the number or ask a reliable student to do this.

8. At higher levels, ask students what values have been discussed. Examples might be fairness, age-equality, and the importance of life experience or education. Ask them which ones are most important to them.

9. Ask students to take notes on any useful language that has come up.

Follow-up
1. Students can use the language that arose, and which is now written on the board, in a role play of a conversation between the man and his disapproving neighbour, or in a written summary of the discussion including their own views and a justification of the views.

2. Students can be given new situations to discuss that reflect their interests and experience. Encourage them to better their score of ideas and reasons each time they discuss (see below for sources of topics and situations).

Variations
A If you wish to help students with ideas for the discussion in step 5, you can provide them with a set of *What if...?* questions to help

6.8 What's the right thing to do?

them think. Examples might be:
- What if the man has lots of very expensive plants that need special care?
- What if the teenager comes from a family without a wage earner?
- What if the retired person used to be a gardener?

These can be provided orally as you monitor any groups having difficulties, or can be written on the board or given out on paper before the group work.

B Alternatively, in step 5 you can provide the groups with sets of statements written on slips of paper. These slips can contain statements of fact, opinions and irrelevant details. Students can move the slips around, prioritise or classify them, or put some to one side, as they wish. If you provide the ideas, as in variation A, then you will not count up student ideas as in the main activity.

C Students can offer ethical dilemmas of their own or can write information relevant to a topic they are given.

D If you would rather not talk about personal moral issues in class, there are many other issues that are likely to spark good discussions. Examples are:
- conspiracy theories (who killed Marilyn Monroe or John F Kennedy? Is Elvis really dead? Did the Americans really walk on the moon or are the pictures a sham?)
- the claims of complementary medicine
- the good and bad things about increased life expectancy.

Alternatively, you can use the same procedure to practise thinking about other people's likely decisions rather than one's own moral stance. Example situations are:
- Bruno is a 14-year-old teenager. Is he going to get a motorbike? or
- The Johnson family live in a suburb. Are they going to get a dog? or
- Sally has to choose her exam subjects. Which ones will she choose?

You can provide *What if ...* questions as in variation A, and/or statements of fact, opinion and irrelevance as in variation B.

Notes

Real life ethical dilemmas can be found by googling 'the ethicist' for collections of Randy Cohen's dilemma columns in the *New York Times* and British *Times* newspapers. The *Times Modern Morals* site is also useful. The web sites have reader comments and the columnist's own

6.8 What's the right thing to do?

view of the right thing to do in the situation (see also Cohen, 2003). Authentic comments can be simplified if necessary, and shared with students after they have produced their own ideas and texts. There is usually strong motivation to read the columns at that stage. If you find these columns too grown-up and sophisticated, try using ethical dilemmas such as:
- Whether some students who lack confidence should get better marks than they deserve, just to encourage them.
- If you should tell your friend or relative the truth when they ask your opinion of clothing they have bought and which you think is awful.

Acknowledgement
Thanks to Lin and Mackay, 2004, for the statements idea in variation B and to Jim Carmichael for the topic ideas in variation D.

6.9 Which proverb is right?

> Making decisions

Focus: Understanding, interpreting and comparing proverbs. Speaking and vocabulary development.

Level: Pre-Intermediate upwards

Time: 5–10 minutes per lesson in several different lessons

Materials/Preparation: You need a set of proverbs (see variations for suggestions). Think up an example win-all or lose-all situation, to illustrate step 3.

in class

1. Introduce the word *proverb* to your students. Make sure they understand it and can give you a few examples in their mother tongue. Ask if they know any English proverbs. If they do, start with one of those, preferably one that is not too old-fashioned and so still carries relevant meaning for them.

2. Read out or write up on the board a proverb, e.g. 'You win some, you lose some'. Help students to understand it and to say it. Ask them to copy it into a special section of their notebooks.

3. Ask students if they think the proverb is true. Then ask them for some example situations from their own lives, where they or someone they know won some and lost some. Ask them for times in the lives of people they know or have heard of, when these people won everything or lost everything. Have an example of your own to offer if students get stuck at this stage.

4. If you feel that there is a proverb in the students' own language that has an extremely similar meaning, remind them of it.

5. Ask students to learn the proverb, its meaning and its pronunciation for homework.

Follow-up

1. In a follow-up lesson, ask the students to recall the proverb dealt with in the earlier lesson. Then introduce another proverb and work with it in the same way.

2. Once you have worked with a few proverbs, you can use them in any of the ways listed below.

6.9 Which proverb is right?

Variations

A   Encourage students to pair up proverbs that are similar in meaning e.g.
- Two heads are better than one – Many hands make light work.

B   Help students to find proverbs that have opposing meanings, e.g.:
- Look before you leap – S/he who hesitates is lost.
- Don't put off until tomorrow what you can do today – Better late than never.

C   Ask students to pair up proverbs that show different aspects of similar topics, e.g.:
- Trouble comes double – It never rains but it pours.

D   Discuss with students which proverbs they think are true/false of themselves or that they need or don't need to heed most.

E   As the class comes across characters in other class material such as stories, encourage them to apply a proverb where appropriate. E.g. if a character drives off too fast in a car and has an accident, you can ask students which of the proverbs she should have thought about before she did it. ('More haste, less speed' and 'Look before you leap.')

F   Ask your students to collect proverbs from different languages translated into English, e.g. 'Recite *patience* three times and it will spare you a murder' (Korea) and 'When money talks, truth keeps silent' (Russia).

Notes
See Strauss, 1994, for more European proverbs.
The internet has many lists of proverbs, some alphabetised, with meanings and origins, by country and by topic area. Type 'proverbs' into the search box.

6.10 Should I do what I am told by famous people?

> Making decisions

Focus: Integrated skills. Interpreting short inspirational texts and considering their application.

Level: Pre-Intermediate upwards

Time: 15 minutes

Materials/Preparation: You need a set of short, inspirational, debatable texts such as quotations (see below for suggestions).

in class

1. Introduce the topic of famous people and how what they say in books, films and speeches sometimes gains popularity. Give or elicit a few easy everyday examples of advertising slogans students might know such as *Just do it*! or political slogans such as *Yes, we can!* You could use catch phrases from TV characters, too, as long as they are examples of exhortations.

2. Write up an inspirational quote that urges people to do something or to do it in a certain way. An example is:
   'Always do what you are afraid to do.' Ralph Waldo Emerson.

   Make sure students understand the quote. You could also say a little about Emerson who was an American essayist, philosopher and poet (1803-1882).

3. Ask students to consider whether the advice in the quote is good or not. Encourage them to come up with example situations when it might be a good idea and others when it might not.

4. Ask students to rewrite the quote so that it expresses what they personally believe is good advice. You may need to go round helping students to express what they want to say. Thus they might write, *If you are afraid, listen to your feelings. You may have good reasons for the fear!* Get them to sign their names after their quote as if they were a famous person. If some students feel that the original quote expresses exactly what they themselves feel and can justify this, then accept this happily.

5. Ask students who have rewritten the original quotation to read out their own quotes and names. Ones that provoke the most

6.10 Should I do what I am told by famous people?

agreement or laughter or are considered the wisest can be stored in a class file or on a poster on the wall together with the original starter quote.

Follow-up
In follow-up lessons, you can work with other quotations in the same way. Here are a few more examples:
- 'Try not to become a person of success but a person of value.' Adapted from Albert Einstein.
- 'Let thy words be few.' Ecclesiastes 5:2.
- 'Silence does not always mark wisdom.' Samuel Taylor Coleridge.
- 'The middle course is the best.' Cleobulus.

Variations

A Students can find their own source quotations and can collect them in different categories such as *Quotations I agree (or disagree) with*, or by topic.

B Students can collect and then compare and contrast quotations on the same topic.

C This sort of work can also be done using short, inspirational poems.

D If students take to this work, you can introduce a thread called *A quote / poem a day (or a week)*, but remember that the main idea is actually to question the advice in the quote or poem.

Notes
If you type 'inspirational quotes' or 'inspirational poems' into your internet search box, you will find many useful sites, such as www.inspirational-quotes.info and www.heartsandminds.org.

6.11 Learning from stories

> Learning from stories

Focus: Helping students to interpret stories and to gain knowledge and perspective from them. Reading, speaking, language development.

Level: Pre-Intermediate upwards

Time: 30 minutes

Materials/Preparation: You need a story that will appeal to students and get them involved. Preparation depends on the way you work with the story (see below for suggestions).

in class

1. Use any of the ideas below to get students interested in the story:
   - Show the title or some pictures or objects, or play some sounds connected to the story, and ask students to guess what the story could be about.
   - Put any key words or phrases necessary for understanding the story up on the board in a random array. Help students to understand them. They then ask Yes/No questions, using the words and phrases, to see if they can guess parts or all of the story.
   - Tell the first part of the story only, and tell them you will finish it later.
   - Give out the bare bones of the story on cut-up slips of paper that students have to order.
   - Give them two stories, but mixed up so that they will have to pull them apart.

2. Use any of the ideas below to reveal the story to the students:
   - Tell some or all of the story to them orally, using prompts to help your memory and so that the telling will be lively.
   - Give out part or all of the story, and let them read it silently in class or at home.
   - Play a video or sound recording of the story.
   - Ask a colleague or friend to come into your class to tell a story.
   - Give out two stories mixed up so that students have to sort them out (see Frank, 1982, pp. 28–32, for such stories). The two stories can be utterly different or can reflect two sides of the same coin, e.g. life on weekdays / life at the weekend; a village after a flood / after reconstruction; a wonderful / terrible holiday.

6.11 Learning from stories

3. Help students to understand the basic meaning of the language in the story in your usual ways, using dictionaries, examples, pictures, gestures, questions, explanations and so on.

4. After most or all of the story has been revealed and the language in it understood, use any of the ideas below:
    - Ask students to think up a good title for the story if it hasn't already got one or if you have hidden it.
    - Draw a time line on the board and ask students to call out events that happened in the order they occurred. Plot key events along the time line.
    - Ask students to dream up alternatives to what happened at key points along the timeline (see activity 4.8 too).
    - Ask students to make up an ending if the story is unfinished. (See Frank, 1982, pp. 78-9, for some stories to finish.)
    - Use Questioning Techniques. Fisher, 2008, pp. 79-86, suggests helping students to ask and answer questions about the following aspects of stories:

Aspects of stories

Contexts
Where and when does the story take place?
Who is in it?
What is the relationship between the characters?
What do the characters feel, think, believe and do, and
Who has power in the story?

Temporal order
What happened at the beginning, in the middle and at the end?
What happened before the story started?
What will happen now it's over?

Particular events
What happened?
Why?
What could have/should have happened?

Intentions
What does X believe / want / want others to think?
What reasons would X give?
What does X hope will happen?

Choices
What is the key moment in the story?
What choices have to be made?
Who has to make the choice?
What could they do?
What would you do?
Did they make the right choice?

Meanings
What is the story about?
Can you think of another title for it?
What does the story tell us?
What is the message / moral of the story?
How is it like / unlike other stories?

The telling
Was there anything special about the story?
Was it well told?
Could you tell this story in a different way?
How would you change the characters or events?

6.11 Learning from stories

Follow-up
Once students see that it's all right to question a story, and see the aspects of stories that can be questioned and the sorts of questions they can ask, encourage them to come up with their own questions in future.

Notes
If you would like to see a professional storyteller in action, look for video clips of Jan Blake on the internet.

See activity 4.8 for reversals stories.

For skeletons of stories that will appeal to adults, see www.businessballs.com/stories.htm.

6.12 Thinking clearly about problems

> Problem solving

Focus: Speaking and listening. Language development related to the situations discussed.

Level: Pre-Intermediate upwards

Time: 20 minutes per lesson over several lessons

Materials/Preparation: You need several problem situations and a list of strategic questions. See below for suggestions for both.

in class

1. Read out, or give students to read, a text about a situation that contains one or more problems, dilemmas or choices. Here is an example:

    Jane won the lottery last winter, and has so much money now that people are always asking her to be their friend and to give them money.

2. Take the first few questions from the list of strategic questions for problem solving in variation A. Work with the questions on the situation you have just stated to the class. Thus, for example, you might ask students these questions:

    - What is the situation? (Students restate it as they understand it.)
    - Is there a problem? (Some students may think not. Others may suggest one.)
    - What would be an even bigger problem? (E.g. Jane having no money at all, Jane being ill, Jane having no friends.)
    - How many problems can we see? (E.g. people know Jane is rich, so she might get mugged. People keep phoning her up; they ask her for money, and this is embarrassing. How much money should she give to whom? Will people get angry if they find out she has given more to one person than to another? Will she give all her money away and have nothing left? Jane does not know if they are friends with her because they like her or because they want her money.)

    It is important not to judge any of the ideas that the students come up with. Simply encourage them to be prolific at this stage.

6.12 Thinking clearly about problems

3. Help students with any language they need as it arises in the lesson.

4. When you have done the amount of work you want for one lesson, write up the questions you have used in the lesson on a poster or other permanent display area. Ask students to note them down, too, together with any useful language that has arisen. Also, record in a lively way ideas that have been suggested by students. See variation B below.

5. Tell students you will continue with the work in a follow-up lesson.

Follow-ups
Ask students to remind you of the basic situation and of the ideas on it so far. Review any useful language. Use the same situation again with the next few questions from the list below. At the end of the lesson, add the questions you have used to the list you have posted up, and make sure students add them to their list too. Keep going over several lessons, until you have tried out all the questions. Ask students in what situations they think this sort of work might be useful to them.

6.12 Thinking clearly about problems

Variations

A Use different questions from the list below in different lessons:

Strategic questions for problem solving

What is the situation?
Is there a problem?
If there is, what would be an even bigger problem?
How many problems can we see?
Can we break them down into smaller problems?
What do we think we know?
Are we assuming anything?
What do we need to find out?
In what different ways can we state the challenges or problem(s)?
In what ways could we resolve the situation?
What do I think?
What does my friend think?
What do we all think?
Can we combine and improve each other's ideas?
How would other people, fictional characters or my heroes go about resolving the problem?
Has anyone anywhere had success with a situation like this in the past?

Can we draw a picture or a diagram of the situation?
Have we all said what we think?
What are the pros, cons and interesting points so far?
Who can think of a different point of view or an alternative?
Can we predict the consequences of the alternatives we have explored so far?
Can we think of a metaphor for the problem?
Can we be more prolific?
What questions can we ask now?
What questions are still unanswered?
How could we be wrong here?
Are there any vested interests?
What are our values?
Can we synthesise all the information?
How do we know which of our solutions is best?
Do we need to move to a decision?
What should we *not* do?

B Record ideas that students come up with by writing phrases in different colours, drawing icons or little diagrams, and storing thoughts under columns headed *What ideas can we use now?* and *What ideas need more work?* on post-it notes or coloured posters. The aim is to make the thoughts visually attractive and to add a different perspective on the situation. (See Michalko, 2001, pp. 23–80, for much more on this.)

6.12 Thinking clearly about problems

C Use different situations and problems in different lessons. Here are some ideas:
- In what ways can I learn more English words?
- How can we stop bullying in schools?
- A divorcee is going to remarry. She has two children from her first marriage. Her future husband has three. They don't have much money. They rent separate small flats at the moment. They are not sure what to do about accommodation.
- The whole world needs bees to pollinate the majority of crops we use to feed people. Bees are getting scarce.

D Add an extra strategic question at the start of the list, which is *Can we find a situation that offers us a challenge?* Then encourage students to come up with situations that they would like to discuss.

Notes
One reason why most of us sigh at the very thought of problems is perhaps because we tend to get locked into one way of looking at a problem and find just one idea that doesn't solve it anyway! As an antidote to this cognitive short circuit, Michalko (2001) recounts an anecdote about Albert Einstein who was reputedly asked what he would do if he was told that in one hour a huge comet would hit and totally destroy the earth. Einstein said he would spend 55 minutes figuring out how to formulate the question of what to do and five minutes solving the problem. Trying not to rush to a solution but instead allowing time to restate a situation and to generate multiple perspectives is thus a major part of the approach advocated by both Einstein and Michalko. This activity is based on this.

For more reasonable and unreasonable problems see Perkins, 2000.

CHAPTER 7
DESIGNING TASKS AND ACTIVITIES TO ENCOURAGE THINKING

In this chapter we will look at five simple principles that can be used with activities in course books and teachers' resource books, with any task you happen to know and regularly use in class, or as a basis for making up new activities of your own. The principles are:
- removing restrictions from activities,
- adding restrictions to activities,
- using classroom formats that encourage thinking and the sharing of ideas,
- choosing interesting themes and materials, and
- using imagination and fantasy.

Teaching Tips

TT1 **Removing restrictions from activities**

Removing restrictions encourages students to think of a number of possible right answers rather than stopping at one, and so helps their reasoning as well as developing language connected to the task.

Take a course book or other exercise, such as a gap fill text. Some gap fill texts provide fillers, in brackets or in lists below the exercise, for students to choose from. They often drive students towards one correct answer. Below is an example. Now simply remove the bank of fillers from the bottom.

Give students the exercise that you have changed. Look at the first gap and discuss together what could go into it. Accept any suggestions that work. So, for example, the words *right, correct, proper, obvious* and *only* will all go in the gap.

Invite students to work alone on the rest of the gaps. Encourage them to think of two or three possible fillings for each gap, in other words, to be prolific.

In pairs, students discuss their suggested fillings, and then as a whole class, discuss which fillings are possible grammatically, which are possible despite changing the meaning or association, and which are absolutely impossible and why.

The history of chocolate
So where and when did the story begin? Thousands of years ago is the ………. answer, in the ………. Maya and Aztec civilizations of Central America.
Cocoa trees grew ………. in the jungle, and people used them to make a ………, drink for ………. occasions. Centuries later the Aztec Empire fell, and Hernán Cortés, the conqueror, brought …… beans back across the seas to Spain.
Gradually chocolate spread across Europe – it was the ………. choice of royalty and the ……, just like caviar or champagne today. At the end of the 19th century milk was added, and at last someone …………. devised a way of making chocolate to eat as well as to drink. But it wasn't until the …………. century that chocolate became ……… for everyone.
So chocolate has been on a(n) ……… journey. Its popularity is ………: prized once by ……….warriors and today by millions of people around the world.

Fillers: Aztec, epic, special, spicy, rich, right, clever, fashionable, enduring, affordable, ancient, cocoa, 20th, wild.

Teaching Tips

Another idea would be to take a matching exercise, such as this one:

The teacher	won a Nobel prize for Physics.
The scientist	came first in the race.
The athlete	gave me a prescription.
The shop assistant	taught English.
The doctor	brought me a pair of shoes.

Instead of asking students to match each job on the left with one obviously connected phrase on the right, remove this restriction and encourage them to match anything with anything as long as they can justify it. So a student may say, 'The teacher came first in the race because she jogs in her free time and entered a half marathon on the weekend.' Accept with good grace and playfulness any offering that is a possible 'unmatch'.

I am grateful to Penny Ur for these suggestions for altering coursebook exercises. Being prolific is one principle for practising creativity (see chapter 6). And activity 1.11 also encourages many right answers.

TT2 Adding restrictions to activities

Here is a way of encouraging students to think their way around exercise restrictions and thus develop language connected to the task. It is suitable for pre-intermediate upwards.

Take any activity or course book exercise and add one or more restrictions to it. Here is a very simple example just to illustrate the idea. Take the task, 'Guess the object I am thinking of!' and add one of the following restrictions or hints, e.g.:
- time ('You only have 30 seconds.'),
- number ('You only have 20 questions.'), or
- context ('It is one of the ones on this list/grid or in this picture.').

Ask the students to guess the object you have in mind, and make a mental note of the questions that they ask as they go along trying to guess the object.

Once the time limit is up, or the number of questions exhausted, depending on the restriction you have applied, or once the object has been correctly guessed, discuss with the students the quality of the questions they asked.

Good quality questions, rather than wild guesses, would be ones that quickly exclude a high proportion of possible guesses. So, if you are working with a picture or a grid, a good quality question would

Teaching Tips

be about location, e.g. 'Is it in the left/right/top/bottom half of the picture/grid?' If you were working with the whole world as your pool of possible objects, then high quality questions could be ones dealing with materials (animal, vegetable, or mineral) or degree of complexity or size or, again, location, e.g. 'Is it in this room?' etc. Similarly, if you asked students to guess a number from 1-1,000, good questions might be: 'Is it more than 500?', 'Is it more than 750?', 'Is it more than 875?'

Do the activity again with a different object or different number in mind to see if students can improve their question quality, so guessing the answer more quickly or with fewer questions, depending on the restriction you apply. Then make sure students are aware of the thinking tool they have been using and the whole idea of high quality questions.

Once students have got the hang of these simple tasks, their restrictions and the ways of getting round these, and can solve the problem without thinking too much, change the restriction or add a novel element or outcome to the task (see below for ideas).

Here are some more categories of restriction that can be applied to language learning activities:
- **Personalisation**: students have to rewrite, respond, ask, or give examples from their own point of view.
- **Thinking of others**: topics such as rooms, holidays, weekends, meals, jobs, daily routines etc can be discussed in terms of how they would differ for the head teacher of your school, the Queen, a homeless person, a skilled craftsperson, a famous pop star, or Posh and Becks.
- **Volume**: students have to give 10 (or 20 or 30 or 40).
- **Student language**: only Yes/No questions are allowed, or students cannot answer yes or no, or sentences must start with each letter of the alphabet one by one (A,B,C,D etc), or utterances can only contain five words etc.
- **Binary decisions**: students have to decide if an item is formal/informal, pretty/ugly, healthy/unhealthy, would suit them/their best friend, is simple/complex, easy/difficult, comic/serious, bland/delicious, true/false, realistic/unrealistic (see Jones and Swarbrick, 2004, pp. 16-22).
- **Change the format**: students need to present information, ideas or opinions in graph, flowchart, mind map, column, or pie chart form.
- **Change the audience and purpose**: information, ideas or opinions need to be rewritten as, e.g., a recipe, weather report, haiku poem, advert, 'how to' manual, or fairy tale.

- **Alter the material or output**: students have to shrink or expand it, add something in or take something out, reverse or transfer it or create something with or from it.
- **Add criteria**: e.g. *unusualness* (students try to give an example that nobody else in the class gives), *persuasiveness* (students try to think of arguments that will persuade their classmates to agree with them), *humour* (if a student gets a laugh from other class members, they get a point).

My thanks to Dr Alexander Sokol, author of the Thinking Approach to language teaching and learning and leader of the TA Group, Riga, Latvia, (www.thinking-approach.org), for alerting me to the principle of adding limitations or restrictions to tasks and to the idea of evaluating the quality of student offerings in order to move students on from typical or no-thinking responses to more thoughtful ones.

TT3 Using classroom formats that encourage thinking and sharing of ideas

It is perfectly possible for students to collaborate and share when sitting in fixed rows of desks. They can work with the person on their left, then on their right, then the person behind, then the one in front. They can pass paper along the rows, and the students at the ends of the rows can write things on posters or carry messages. However, there follow four different classroom formats we can employ that use physical arrangements to advantage in encouraging thinking and the sharing of ideas between students.

A **Think pair share** (see Lyman, 1981)
This idea can be used at any level, in classes of any number and with any physical layout. Students first work individually on a task. They concretise their thoughts in some way, such as by committing them to paper in note form. Next, each student works with one other person to pool their ideas using their notes to help them. If you have an odd number of students, you will need to have one trio. Working with another student gives each one practice in expressing their own ideas and, usually, helps them to add ideas to their own list. Finally, in plenary, the teacher encourages open sharing in the whole class. Students have already gained confidence in their pairs and so usually feel able to offer ideas out loud in the group at this stage. The pair can also see how they stand as to the number, quality and type of ideas produced alone and in their pair, compared to those produced by others in the group.

Teaching Tips

B Individual roles

This idea works with students at any level, in pairs and in groups of any number. Students are given different roles to perform. It can actually help to reduce the noise levels of group work if one or more of the students has a listening or watching brief as an Observer. Other roles a student or pair of students of the same or different levels can be given are: prompter (for when people run out of ideas or language), questioner, summariser, host(ess) (to make sure everyone speaks) and tester or reviewer. The roles can be discussed in the whole class first and then, written on slips of paper, handed to individual students or to pairs of students. For example, a higher level student working with a pair of lower level students can be given a slip of paper saying *Observer*. This student can also get a list of, for example, the phrases the pair could use in the role play dialogue they are about to do. During the pair work, every time the higher level student hears one of the phrases being used, s/he can tick it off the list. After the role play, the observer can give feedback to the pair on which items were used or not used, or who used most, or how well they were pronounced.

C The teaching learning wheel

This idea works well with intermediate level groups. Pairs or trios sit at separate tables. Each pair or trio has a different section of a text or different diagram, picture, story, or list of words depending on what you want the students to study and learn. The task stays on the same table throughout the activity. Give students a time limit and start them off. Each of the pairs or trios studies, discusses, learns or memorises the subject matter on their table. After the time is up, one person from the pair or group stays at the table while the other(s) move in a clockwise direction to a new table. Once people are settled, give a time limit. The student who stayed behind now teaches or explains the subject matter on their table to those who have just moved to their table. These newly formed pairs or trios study, discuss and learn as before, using the material that has stayed on the table.

Once the time is up, the person in each group who stayed put last time now moves in a clockwise direction to a new table. Those who moved last time stay put this time. Thus the ones who stayed last time catch up with their old friends. Once people are settled, again set a time limit. As before, the pairs and trios work on the subject matter on their table. The activity goes on in this way. So, one time one individual stays at a table while the other one(s) move. Next time, the one who stayed moves and catches up with their colleague(s). Keep going until the pairs or trios have studied, discussed and learned all the material you wish them to. (Thanks to Chambers, 2002, for this idea)

D Merry-go-round
This idea works well with large groups. Divide your class up so that you have equal numbers of groups and group members so, e.g., if you have 16 students, make four groups of four. If you have 25, make five groups of five. If you have 36 students, make six groups of six. Get as near to this as you can. Give each group a station or a table where they will stay throughout the activity. Each group is then given a different task but related to the same topic. Examples could be:
- House Vocabulary. Each group has a different room to gather words for.
- A discussion of the advantages and disadvantages of living in the city versus in the country. Each group has a different part to prepare.

Hand out a large sheet of thick paper and some thick dark pens to each group. The first thing each group must do is copy its task clearly onto the top of one of the large sheets of thick paper. Then give them a time limit in which to discuss the task and to write notes on the sheet of paper on which they wrote the task. Explain that their writing needs to be clear but not too big, as others are going to read their notes and also add notes onto the same piece of paper.

When the time is up, and at a pre-arranged signal, ask people to stop talking and writing. Each group now passes the sheet of paper, with the task and the notes they have written on it, in a clockwise direction to the next table. (If you wish, one person can travel as the task's 'ambassador' to the next table.) This means that each table now receives a new piece of paper with a fresh task on it and some thoughts already written on it (and, if you wish, an ambassador who can explain any difficulties).

Each group now reads this fresh task and the notes from the previous group and discusses the topic. They add what they can to the sheet in the time available. Thus, after each study and discussion time, the task sheet and connected written notes are passed clockwise to the next group. There will be a little more reading to do each time the paper travels, as there will be more and more writing on the large sheet of paper. Have some spare sheets in case students run out of space. (Thanks to Chambers, 2002, for this idea.)

If you wish, as well as the role of ambassador, students can be given or choose to take on one of the following roles: target language checker (the person who encourages people to speak in the target language and writes down in mother tongue the things classmates don't know how to say in English), dictionary person (the one who looks up words). (See also 'Individual roles in the group', activity B above.)

Once all the groups have seen, discussed and written notes on all or the majority of the tasks, you can bring the group work to a close and ask students to hang up all the sheets of paper, using clothes pegs, onto a clothes line you have strung across a corner of the classroom. Students can then come and read the accumulated wisdom.

TT4 Choosing interesting themes and material types

If we want to have interesting thoughts, one thing that can help us is to have interesting things to think about and interesting materials to work with. We do need to discover what students find interesting. But if we stick only to those topics dear to their hearts, things might get a bit repetitive. Equally well, if we only work with topics that we teachers find interesting, we may lose our students all together. A mixture of student choice, teacher choice and ideas from the list below might help!

A Some of the topics that have come up in this book so far have been:
Handshakes, cats, colours, my room, my favourite object, body piercing, lying, wild animals, ground rules for good conversations, school rules, shopping, buttons, ethics, Cinderella, new inventions, creativity, potatoes, guerrilla gardening, the principles of good design, metaphors and the history of chocolate.

B Other possible topics are:
Sign language, how to make a really good sand castle, whether girls or boys have it easier, if zoos are good or bad for the preservation of animal species, if school breaks should be shorter, the good things about homework, who and where each one of us was three/five months/years ago, who and where each one of us will be one month/year/decade from now, why stars twinkle, what bad habits we have, who wants to escape, what from, where to and with whom, superstitions, forbidden fruit, dreams, memories, sharing, high-wire walking, virtuosity, how the heart works, if volcanoes are important. (Thanks to Peter Grundy, 1989, for some of these topics and for thoughts on unusual ways of using them.)

C Some materials that are naturally engaging and stimulating to work with are:
Textiles, films, books, sea shells, video clips, quotations, proverbs, internet images, stories, cartoons, tweets, instrumental music, very short newspaper articles, posters, sounds, strange or unusual objects, art reproductions, student drawings, problems, poems, dialogue journals, photos, problem page letters from age-relevant publications, adverts, smells of herbs and spices, pressed flowers, icons, junk mail, mobile phones and digital cameras. It's a good idea to make sure we use a variety of such materials.

Teaching Tips

TT5 **Using imagination and fantasy**

If you are a busy working teacher with a full timetable plus marking, meetings and preparation, you may not have the time or energy to let your imagination run riot and to invent totally new exercises and activities yourself. There are, however, some very interesting radio and TV programmes that we can all use to inspire the creation of fun, useful activities for our classes. Now that the BBC has a very useful web site with podcasts and 'listen again' facilities, it is easy to use these programmes with students whose level is high enough. Ideas that I personally have enjoyed and then turned into useful classroom activities include very long-running shows such as *Desert Island Discs* (which practises vocabulary, opinions and preferences language as well as prioritising) *Call My Bluff* (useful for vocabulary work) and *Just a Minute* (good for spontaneity and oral fluency).

From within comedy shows comes the idea of a caption contest, where students think of amusing captions for strange or funny pictures, and 'How Many Questions can you Think of for this Answer?'. In this last activity, students are given answers such as *Five* or *Not very often* and have to think of as many possible questions to match the answer as they can. So, for *Five* they could say, 'How many weekdays are there?' 'How many fingers are there on one hand?' 'How many feet tall is Alex?' 'How many millions would you like to win on the lottery?' 'How many kittens has the cat had?' 'What time did you get home from school?' Caption Contest and 'How Many Questions can you Think of?' push students to be prolific as well as creative and amusing.

Activities 7.1 and 7.2 are based on ideas adapted from radio and TV programmes running in the UK at the time of writing.

7.1 The Museum of Curiosities

> An adaptation of a UK radio programme

Focus: The language of description and persuasion. Discussion language. Integrated skills.

Level: Pre-Intermediate upwards

Time: 20 minutes in the first lesson followed by homework and 20 minutes in each follow-up lesson.

Materials/Preparation: You need to think of three or four items you would like to put in an imaginary museum. See step 2 for examples.

in class

1. Explain to the class that they are going to build an exhibition in an imaginary museum. The museum has infinite space and infinite amounts of money so the exhibits in it can be gigantic, microscopic, expensive, strange or even unreal! They can be a person, a thing or an abstract concept. Each time you work on the museum, four people will form an advisory committee. Each member of the committee will suggest one exhibit, and will explain why the exhibit should go into the museum. The class will vote on whether to accept each exhibit or not. The final decision will rest with you, the teacher.

2. Start the museum off by suggesting a couple of exhibits yourself. Choose things which are objectively impossible, such as all the pets you have ever owned, or the moon and the stars, or the teddy bear you lost when you were ten, or your kitchen or Sandi Toksvig. Describe each exhibit carefully and say why you would like it to be in the museum. Let students ask you questions about each exhibit. Encourage them to express their reasons for thinking it would be a good or bad idea for the museum (remember, space and price are not a problem).

3. Put each of your exhibits to a class vote. If something does not get in, accept it with good grace if you get good reasons. If something gets in, again for good reasons, make a note of this and ask students to make a 'Museum' section in their notebooks and then write down the name of the exhibit, the donor (you) and a short description of the item in it.

7.1 The Museum of Curiosities

4. Ask students to think of some exhibits they could offer to the museum in the follow-up lesson. As the ideas come up in class, discuss a couple with the students straight away, but don't vote on them yet.

5. Set the homework, which is for the first four students to prepare a description of an exhibit each, with reasons why they think it should be included. If possible, they should discuss their possible offerings with each other before finally choosing so as to avoid overlaps and get a good variety to put to the rest of the class in the follow-up lesson.

Follow-up
1. Invite the four members of the museum advisory committee to come to sit at the front of the class. Each of them describes their imaginary exhibit in turn and says why they would advise that it be included in the museum. The rest of the class can ask questions and discuss each exhibit before moving to a vote. You can override a vote only if you have very good reasons and can explain them to the class. All exhibits that are accepted should be listed, together with the name of the donor and a brief description, in the special section of student notebooks. When the writing phase is over, choose the members of the next advisory committee for a follow-up lesson.

2. The imaginary museum will gradually build as exhibits are added to it. Students can then start to add criteria for accepting new exhibits such as 'Really different from anything else in the museum so far'.

Variations
A Each time you work on the museum, you can have between one and five students on your advisory committee, depending how much time you would like to devote to the activity each time and over what time period.

B Once there are some exhibits in the museum, students can design an imaginary set of buildings and spaces, decide how to arrange the different exhibits, make special spaces or wings for various themes, explain the idea to their family and friends, and 'bring in' their exhibits to add to those of the class, or design and produce a catalogue of exhibits.

Acknowledgement
This idea was inspired by a BBC Radio programme of the same name.

7.2 Room 101

> An adaptation of a UK TV programme

Focus: Speaking and listening. Expressing dislikes and reasons. Vocabulary development. Discussion language.

Level: Pre-Intermediate upwards

Time: 20 minutes each lesson over a few lessons

Materials/Preparation: You need to think of one pet hate that you would like to consign to Room 101. See below for examples.

in class

1. Tell students that there is a special place in the world called 'Room 101'. It is a bit like hell. Once something gets in there it can never get out. It may be burnt or drowned or destroyed in some way. So Room 101 is a great place to put things that annoy you. However, what annoys you might be precious to someone else. So it is really important to discuss whatever you want to put in there very carefully before you close the door and it disappears for ever. If you wish, you can add exclusions such as 'You can't put people you know in Room 101'.

2. Suggest an idea of your own to put in Room 101, e.g. people who talk on their mobile phones on the train, English mustard, Mathematics or the jingle from the Coca Cola advert. Say why the thing irritates you and why you think it should be gone for ever.

3. Put students into threes to discuss your idea and to think of questions to ask about it, and arguments against it.

4. Ask students to quarrel with you! Someone might say, 'Maybe it's an emergency and someone needs to talk on the mobile phone on the train'. Or, 'If you don't like it, you can move to another part of the train.' Accept good arguments with grace. If students come up with really good arguments, you can change your mind and decide you don't want to put the item you proposed into Room 101 after all. Or, after plenty of discussion, move to a vote. If your item is NOT allowed to go into Room 101, accept this in very good humour. If it is, everyone should make a note that it is now in Room 101. Other items may be added in later lessons.

7.2 Room 101

5. For homework, students are to think of some things they would like to consign to Room 101 and be prepared to explain why to the class another time.

Follow-up

1. Students can make a cardboard box painted black or with orange flames on it to symbolise Room 101. Slips of paper with items written on can then be popped in whenever something is voted in.

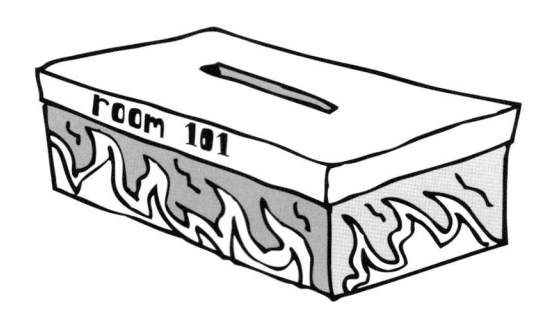

2. In later lessons students propose things to go into Room 101, explain why, discuss, argue and then move to a vote.

Note
Room 101 was originally a room at the BBC in which the author George Orwell had to sit through long, boring meetings. In his novel *1984*, Room 101 was the name he gave to a torture chamber. It then became the name of a BBC Radio and TV programme in which celebrities tried to get rid of their pet hates and least favourite places, people or pop songs. Once consigned to Room 101 these pet hates were unable to irritate the celebrity (or anyone else) further.

Further reading

Arnold, J, H Puchta and M Rinvolucri (2007) *Imagine That!: mental imagery in the EFL classroom* Helbling Languages

Ausubel, D (1968) *Educational Psychology: a cognitive view* Holt, Rinehart & Winston

Bloom, B (1956) *Taxonomy of Educational Objectives Handbook 1 The Cognitive Domain* David McKay Co Inc

Bowker, S (2007) *100+ Ideas for Teaching Thinking Skills* Continuum International Publishing Group

Brown, G and E C Wragg (1993) *Questioning* Routledge

Bruner, J (1986) *Actual Minds, Possible Worlds* Harvard University Press

Buzan, T (1993) *The Mind Map Book* BBC Books

Chambers, R (2002) *Participatory Workshops* Earthscan

Cohen, M (2003) *101 Ethical Dilemmas* Routledge

Costa, A and B Kallick (2000) *Habits of Mind: discovering and exploring* Association for Supervision and Curriculum Development

Cotton, K 'Teaching thinking skills' Northwest Regional Educational Laboratory's School Improvement Research Series website www.nwel.org/scpd/sirs/6/cu11.html 1991

Cranmer, D and C Laroy (1992) *Musical Openings* Longman

Dobbs, J (2001) *Using the Board in the Language Classroom* Cambridge University Press

Doidge, N (2007) *The Brain that Changes Itself* Penguin

Feuerstein, R (1980) *Instrumental Enrichment: intervention programme for cognitive modifiability* University Park Press

Fisher, R (1996) *Stories for Thinking* Nash Pollock Publishing

Fisher, R (1997) *Poems for Thinking* Nash Pollock Publishing

Fisher, R (2008) *Teaching Thinking* third edition, Continuum International Publishing Group

Frank, C et al (1982) *Challenge to Think* Oxford University Press

Gagne, R M (1985) *Conditions of Learning* second edition, Holt, Rinehart & Winston

Gerngross, G, H Puchta and S Thornbury (2006) *Teaching Grammar Creatively* Helbling Languages

Gilbert, I (2007) *The Little Book of Thunks* Crown House

Further reading

Gordon, T (2003) *Teacher Effectiveness Training* Three Rivers Press

Grundy, P (1989) 'When will they ever learn?' in *The Teacher Trainer* pp. 4-11 Pilgrims

Hirsch Jr. E D (2010) 'How to save our schools' in the *New York Review of Books* vol. LVII no. 8

Johnstone, K (1981) *Impro* Methuen

Jones, B and A Swarbrick (2004) *It Makes You Think! Creating engagement, offering challenges* CILT

Keddie, J (2008) 'Images 6' in *English Teaching Professional 54* pp. 29-31

Laroy C (1992) *Musical Openings* Longman

Leat, D (2008) 'An interview on thinking skills' in *The Teacher Trainer* vol 21/2 pp. 23-4 Pilgrims

Leicester, M (2010) *Teaching Critical Thinking Skills* Continuum International Publishing Group

Lima, C (2009) 'Interview on critical literacy and global issues' in *The Teacher Trainer* vol 23/2 pp. 10-11 Pilgrims

Lin, M and C Mackay (2004) *Thinking through Modern Foreign Languages* Chris Kington Publishing

Lindstromberg, S (1988) 'Teacher echoing' in *The Teacher Trainer* vol 2/1 p. 18 Pilgrims

Lindstromberg, S (2004) *Language Activities for Teenagers* Cambridge University Press

Lymnan, F (1981) 'The responsive classroom discussion' in Anderson, A S (ed), *Mainstreaming Digest*, University of Maryland College of Education

Margulies N and C Valenza (2005) *Visual Thinking* Crown House

Mercer, N (2000) *Words and Minds* Routledge

Michalko, M (2001) *Cracking Creativity* Ten Speed Press

Miller, G A (1956) *The Magical Number Seven, Plus or Minus Two: Some Limits on our Capacity for Processing Information* in Psychological Review, 63, 81-97

Morgan, J and M Rinvolucri (1983) *Once Upon a Time: using stories in the language classroom* Cambridge University Press

Morgan, N and J Saxton (2002) *Asking Better Questions* second edition, Pembroke Pubs

Further reading

Moseley, D, S Higgins, J Miller, D Newton, J Elliott and M Gregson (2005) *Frameworks for Thinking* Cambridge University Press

Murphey, T (2006) *Language Hungry!* Helbling Languages

Nottingham, J (2010) *Challenging Learning* John Nottingham Publications Ltd, Northumberland

O'Brien, D (2005) *How to Develop a Brilliant Memory Week by Week* Duncan Band Publishers

Paley, V 'On Listening to What Children Say' *Harvard Educational Review* 56(2) 1986

Paran, A (2003) 'Helping Learners to Become Critical: how coursebooks can help' in Renandya, N (ed) *Methodology and Materials Design in Language Teaching* SEAMEO RELC

Perkins, D N (2000) *Archimedes' Bathtub: the art and logic of breakthrough thinking* W W Norton & Company

Pugliese, C (2010) *Being creative* Delta Publications

Reynolds, R (2008) *On Guerrilla Gardening* Bloomsbury

Rinvolucri, M and C Frank (1990) *Grammar in Action* Prentice Hall

Romiszowski, A J (1981) *Designing Instructional Systems: decision making in course planning and curriculum design* Kogan Page

Rowe, M B (1978) *Teaching Science as Continuous Enquiry* McGraw–Hill

Sayed, M (2010) 'How a suburban street in Reading became a wellspring of champions' in *The Week* Issue 765 pp. 52–3

Smith, G F (2004) 'Thinking skills', in Wragg, E C (ed) *Teaching and Learning* Routledge/Falmer reader (ch. 8, pp. 105–22)

Spencer, D H (1967) *Guided Composition Exercises* Longman

Stahl, G (2010) 'Group Cognition as a Foundation for the New Science of Learning' in M S Khine & I M Saleh (eds) *New Science of Learning: Cognition, Computers and Collaboration in Education* Springer

Strauss, E (1994) *Dictionary of European Proverbs* 3 vols. Routledge

Thacker, J (1991) in Gough, D *Thinking about Thinking* USA National Association of Elementary School Principals

Tsai, B and J Feher (2004) *Creative Resources* International Alliance for Learning

Warburton, N (1996) *Thinking from A to Z* Routledge

Further reading

Williams, M and R Burden (1997) *Psychology for Language Teachers* Cambridge University Press

Woodward, T (2001) *Planning Lessons and Courses* Cambridge University Press

Woodward, T (2003) 'Let There Be You. Let There Be Me' in *Folio* vol 8 1/2 pp. 13–14

Woodward, T (2005) 'Mapping the Work Done' in *Ways of Working with Teachers* TW Publications, Elmstone, Kent

Woodward, T (2006) *Headstrong: a book of thinking frames for mental exercise* TW Publications, Elmstone, Kent

Woodward, T (2008–9) 'I Think, Therefore I Learn' a series of five articles in *English Teaching Professional* issue nos 58–62 inclusive

Wragg, E C and G Brown (1993) *Explaining* Routledge

Zimbardo, P and J Boyd (2008) *The Time Paradox* Routledge

Teacher's quick-reference guide

This guide will help you select an activity suitable for your class based on the time you have available and the learning level(s) of your students, and other factors such as the content and language focus.

To use it, look down the left-hand column under a particular chapter till you come to a time that's suitable for you, and then look across to see the name of the activity spread across the range of levels it's suited to. Then across again to find the content focus, the language focus and the activity number. Where the content and/or language focus are blank, the choice is yours.

If you prefer to start with the level of your students, find the level on the top line, then go downwards till you find an activity name, and on that same row you will find the time required, the content focus and language focus, and the activity number.

Please note that the guidance is very basic; it allows you to see, when you're thinking of running an activity for the first time, how long the activity is likely to take according to the author's experience. You're free to change the time, or indeed the level, of any activity according to your preference.

Teacher's quick-reference guide

Lesson time (mins)	Beginner	Elementary	Pre-Intermediate	Intermediate Advanced	Content focus	Language focus	Activity no
Chapter 1 Fundamentals							
2–3	'Menu' on the board	'Menu' on the board	'Menu' on the board	'Menu' on the board	Seeing where we are going	Plans	1.9
5	Clem's spiral	Clem's spiral	Clem's spiral	Clem's spiral	Calm down		1.5
5	Taking the register	Taking the register	Taking the register	Taking the register	Starting a lesson well	Simple dialogue	1.15
5		What? How? Why?	What? How? Why?	What? How? Why?	Ending a lesson well		1.18
5				Transfer	Ending a lesson well		1.19
5–10	Counting games	Counting games	Counting games	Counting games	Wake-up	Numbers	1.3
5–10	Labelling the room	Labelling the room	Labelling the room	Labelling the room	Thinking in English	Room and furniture vocabulary	1.13
5–10		Solo silent reflection	Solo silent reflection	Solo silent reflection	Ending a lesson well		1.16
10		Invent a handshake	Invent a handshake	Invent a handshake	Wake-up	Physical action verbs	1.1
10		Simply stimulate	Simply stimulate	Simply stimulate	Wake-up	Fluency	1.2
10		Concept map	Concept map	Concept map	Seeing where we are going		1.10
10			Crazy questions *or* 'thunks'	Crazy questions *or* 'thunks'	Starting to think up ideas	Justification language	1.11
10–15	Expanding a sentence	Expanding a sentence	Expanding a sentence	Expanding a sentence	Wake-up	Syntax	1.4
10–15	My favourite mistakes	My favourite mistakes	My favourite mistakes	My favourite mistakes	Mistakes are useful	Error correction	1.7
15	My favourite mistakes				Thinking in English	Simple dialogues about classroom situations	1.14
15	Keyword group mapping	Keyword group mapping	Keyword group mapping	Keyword group mapping	Ending a lesson well		1.17
15–20	The learning dip and rise	The learning dip and rise	The learning dip and rise	The learning dip and rise	Learning takes time		1.6
Variable	Just one good thing	Just one good thing	Just one good thing	Just one good thing	Positivity	Past Simple, Present Perfect	1.8
Variable	Puzzles	Puzzles	Puzzles	Puzzles	Thinking up ideas		1.12
Chapter 2 Building concepts, looking for patterns and memorising							
1–3		Mnemonics	Mnemonics	Mnemonics	Memorising	Topic Vocabulary	2.12
5–7		Concept stretching	Concept stretching	Concept stretching	Ensuring and developing understanding		2.4

Teacher's quick-reference guide

Lesson time (mins)	Beginner	Elementary	Pre-Intermediate	Intermediate Advanced	Content focus	Language focus	Activity no
Chapter 2 Building concepts, looking for patterns and memorising							
5-10			Concept sheets		Considering progress		2.3
5-10			Things of this shape		Looking for patterns	Vocabulary of shapes	2.6
5-10			Clap, listen, clap		Recognising sound patterns	Word and sentence stress	2.8
5-10		Rehearsal			Memorising		2.13
5-15		Small collections			Looking for patterns	Building vocabulary	2.7
10				Learning a language is like …?	Developing a long-term view		2.1
10			Question matrix		Working out what questions to ask	Question formation	2.2
10			Physical storage		Building concepts, memorising		2.11
10			Mime round the circle		Memorising, teambuilding	Building vocabulary	2.14
20-40			Guided picture composition		Memorising	Past Simple and connectors	2.16
25			Refining vocabulary		Building concepts	Reinforcing new vocabulary	2.5
30			Eight-step memorising		Memorising		2.15
30-60			Odd one(s) out		Looking for patterns	Building vocabulary, opinions, comparison and contrast, reasoning	2.9
30-60				Like WHAT??!!	Looking for patterns	Topic vocabulary, Past Simple and connectors	2.10
Chapter 3 Keeping it practical							
10			Gathering exploratory talk language		Exploratory talk		3.2
20			Exploratory talk ground rules		Good conversation(s)	Speaking and listening	3.1
25				Inspiring people	Associating with our heroes	Research, reading, writing.	3.4

Teacher's quick-reference guide

Lesson time (mins)	Beginner	Elementary	Pre-Intermediate	Intermediate	Advanced	Content focus	Language focus	Activity no
Chapter 3 Keeping it practical								
30			Doing exploratory talk	Doing exploratory talk		Exploratory talk	Speaking and listening	3.3
30				Behold the humble button!	Behold the humble button!	Associating with our heroes	Describing objects and processes; comparatives	3.5
Chapter 4 Using everyday thinking frameworks								
10		I'm grateful for …	I'm grateful for …			Listing; positivity	Developing vocabulary	4.2
10		Right name wrong name	Right name wrong name			Reversals	Speaking, listening and vocabulary	4.7
20			How times have changed!	How times have changed!		Listing	Past Simple, *used to*, Present Perfect Present Simple, speaking and listening	4.4
20		List poems	List poems	List poems		Listing		4.6
20			That's not right! *or* 'Cinderfella'			Reversals; correcting the teacher	Listening, storytelling	4.8
20			Reversals anecdotes			Reversals	Language of opposites	4.9
20			Working backwards from goals			Reversals	Planning	4.10
20				Fortunately, unfortunately		Reversals	Spontaneous storytelling, listening and speaking	4.11
20				Change the text		Reversals	Reading; adjectives	4.12
30			Rules for a good society			Listing	Topic vocabulary and imperatives	4.1
30				True or false *or* Facts and myths		Listing	Discussion; Present Simple practice	4.3
30				Flip it and see		Reversals	Speaking; present simple; vocabulary development	4.13

Teacher's quick-reference guide

Lesson time (mins)	Beginner	Elementary	Pre-Intermediate	Intermediate Advanced	Content focus	Language focus	Activity no
Chapter 4 Using everyday thinking frameworks							
10 + 20			Are we the same or different?		Listing	Comparison, holiday vocabulary	4.5
Chapter 5 Creative thinking							
10			Creative brainstorm		Being prolific	Vocabulary of creativity; speaking and listening	5.1
10		Checking vocabulary many ways			Being prolific	Vocabulary	5.6
10		Scrabble word review			Making thinking visible	Reviewing associated words	5.9
10–20		Graphic organiser variety			Visual aids		5.11
15			You can use it to …		Being prolific	Vocabulary of everyday objects	5.2
15		Just one colour			Being prolific	Vocabulary development	5.3
15			Thirty things I did		Being prolific	Past Simple	5.4
15				If she were an animal she'd be a panther!	Unusual combinations	Second conditional, speaking, listening and writing	5.8
20			Picture pack plethora		Being prolific	Vocabulary, speaking and writing	5.5
20			Comparing a text and a picture		Unusual combinations	Topic language	5.7
20			Musical post cards		Making thinking visible	Vocabulary and writing postcards	5.10
20			Inventing new buttons		Using a creativity tool	Shapes, materials. Adjective word order.	5.12
20			Potato talks		Using a generative framework	Talking about a given topic, speaking and listening	5.13
20				Acrostics	Using a generative framework	Speaking and listening	5.14

Teacher's quick-reference guide

Lesson time (mins)	Beginner	Elementary	Pre-Intermediate	Intermediate Advanced	Content focus	Language focus	Activity no
Chapter 5 Creative thinking							
20			Two similarities, two differences		Building empathy	Comparisons	5.15
20				I am one among many	Building empathy, informal surveys	Questions, *most of us, none of us*	5.16
20				What are they really thinking?	Building empathy, adverts	Topic vocabulary, speaking, listening, writing	5.18
20			Your festival or mine?		Building empathy, festivals	Questions, Present Simple, vocabulary	5.20
30				Questions to the head	Building empathy	Personal questions, speaking and listening	5.17
30				Half a conversation	Building empathy	Natural dialogue	5.19
Chapter 6 Thinking clearly about texts and situations							
5–10			Which proverb is right?		Understanding proverbs	Speaking, listening, vocabulary development	6.9
15				General knowledge building	Finding out	Questions, reading and topic language	6.7
15			Should I do what I am told by famous people?		Making decisions about behaviour	Reading and interpreting texts	6.10
20			Where does it come from?		Investigating the provenance of a text	Question formation	6.1
20			Spot the smuggled mistake!		Checking veracity of texts	Question formation	6.4
20				What's the right thing to do?	Moral dilemma	Opinions, *should, ought to*, vocabulary development	6.8
20			Thinking clearly about problems		Problem solving	Speaking and listening	6.12

Teacher's quick-reference guide

Lesson time (mins)	Beginner	Elementary	Pre-Intermediate	Intermediate Advanced	Content focus	Language focus	Activity no
Chapter 6 Thinking clearly about texts and situations							
30				Balancing the books	Finding imbalance in texts	Scanning	6.2
30			Fact or opinion?		Identifying differences between fact and opinion	Topic language	6.3
30			Which text is right?		Points of view, facts, opinions	Reading, speaking.	6.5
30				Through my eyes or Am I biased?	Deeply rooted personal opinions	Discussion language, vocabulary development	6.6
30			Learning from stories		Learning from stories	Reading, speaking and listening	6.11
Chapter 7 Designing tasks and activities to encourage thinking							
20			The Museum of Curiosities		Beloved objects	Description and persuasion	7.1
20			Room 101		Pet hates	Likes, dislikes and reasons why	7.2